Ways of Knowing in Science Series
RICHARD DUSCHL, SERIES EDITOR

ADVISORY BOARD: Charles W. Anderson, Nancy Brickhouse,
Rosalind Driver, Eleanor Duckworth, Peter Fensham, William Kyle,
Roy Pea, Edward Silver, Russell Yeany

How Students (Mis-)Understand Science and Mathematics

INTUITIVE RULES

RUTH STAVY and DINA TIROSH

Teachers College, Columbia University
New York and London

Published by Teachers College Press, 1234 Amsterdam Avenue, New York, NY
10027

Library of Congress Cataloging-in-Publication Data

Stavy, Ruth.
   How students (mis-)understand science and mathematics : intuitive rules /
Ruth Stavy and Dina Tirosh.
      p. cm. — (Ways of knowing in science series)
   Includes bibliographical references and index.
   ISBN 0-8077-3959-6 (cloth : alk. paper) — ISBN 0-8077-3958-8 (pbk. :
alk. paper)
      1. Science—Study and teaching.   2. Mathematics—Study and teaching.
3. Cognitive learning.   I. Title: How students misunderstand science and
mathematics.   II. Tirosh, Dina.   III. Title.   IV. Series.
   Q181 .S694   2000
      507'.1—dc21   00-032560

ISBN 0-8077-3958-8 (paper)
ISBN 0-8077-3959-6 (cloth)

Printed on acid-free paper
Manufactured in the United States of America

07 06 05 04 03 02 01 00   8 7 6 5 4 3 2 1

Contents

Introduction

A major thrust in mathematics and science education recently has been the study of students' conceptions and reasoning in science and mathematics. Many have pointed out the persistence of misconceptions, naive conceptions, alternative conceptions, intuitive conceptions, and preconceptions. Studies have covered a wide range of subject areas in physics (astronomy, mechanics, electricity, heat, light, the particulate nature of matter), in chemistry (mole concept, equilibrium), in biology (growth, health, photosynthesis, heredity), and in mathematics (function, infinity, area). (For surveys of students' conceptions, see Confrey, 1990; Driver, 1994; Driver, Guesne, & Tiberghien, 1985; Eylon & Lynn, 1988; Fischbein, 1987; Hart, 1981; Osborne & Freyberg, 1985; Perkins & Simmons, 1988). Most of this research has been content-specific and concerned to provide detailed descriptions of specific alternative concepts (Thijs & van den Berg, 1995).

In view of the volume of documented instances of alternative conceptions, preconceptions, and misconceptions in science and mathematics, a theoretical description covering categorization, general sources, and appropriate educational approaches would seem to be in order. Such a theory should have both explanatory and predictive power: It should enable researchers and teachers to foresee students' inappropriate reactions to specific situations in science and mathematics.

In our work in both mathematics and science education, we have observed that students react in similar ways to a wide variety of scientifically unrelated situations. Although these situations differ with regard either to their content area and/or to the type of reasoning required, they share some common, external features. Based on our observations, we have proposed a theory to explain and predict students' responses to mathematics and scientific tasks: the theory of intuitive rules. Many responses that the literature describes as alternative conceptions could be interpreted as evolving from several common, intuitive rules. We have so far identified three such rules. The first chapter of this book describes and discusses the first rule: "More A–More B." The second does the same regarding the second rule: "Same A–Same B." The third chapter concerns the third rule: "Everything can be divided." The fourth chapter discusses the nature of intuitive rules and their role in our reasoning. To conclude, the fifth chapter deals with educational implications of the intuitive rules.

Acknowledgment

We would like to thank Alice Zilcha, Mirjam Hadar, and Nava Azhari for their assistance and dedication in bringing the manuscript of this book to completion.

How Students (Mis-)Understand Science and Mathematics

INTUITIVE RULES

1

How Children and Adults Use the Intuitive Rule "More A–More B"

There are many situations in everyday life in which we have to compare quantities and determine whether or not they are equal.

How do we make such judgments?
What factors affect our judgments in such situations?

In some cases, it is immediately obvious that, in respect to the quantity in question, one object is equal to or larger than the other. For instance, in the case of two sticks that are identical in all aspects except that one of them is longer than the other, even very young children find the difference in length obvious. This judgment is based on direct visual information.

Often, however, direct perceptual cues are not available. In these cases we may rely on another quantity in order to make the target comparison. For instance, in the case of two identical bottles, one full of milk and the other half-full, it is obvious to young children that the first contains more milk because they perceive the higher level of milk in it. Here, the judgment about the relative quantities of milk is based on the perceived levels of milk in the two bottles. Children from very early on correctly argue that "the higher the level of milk–the more milk we have."

In the above case, the quantity children refer to, *level of milk*, is indeed relevant to the judgment about the relative *quantities of milk*. Everyday life offers many opportunities in which a perceptual quantity (A) can serve as a criterion for comparing another quantity (B). In these cases, "More A (the perceptual quantity) implies More B (the quantity in question)." Quantity A, however, is not always relevant to the required comparison or cannot, by itself, serve as a criterion. For example, when young children compare two cups containing equal amounts of water, with one cup being narrower and taller than the other, they often incorrectly claim that "the taller–the more" (Piaget, 1952/1965).

Studies of the development of students' conceptions in science and mathematics frequently use comparison tasks (see, for instance, Piaget's work on children's conceptions of number, quantity of matter, area, etc.). Children's responses to such comparison tasks are often of the type described above, namely, "More A–More B." For instance, studies of the development of the concept of temperature showed that when children were presented with two cups of warm water, one containing twice as much water as the other, they claimed that "the more water–the warmer" (Brook, Briggs, Bell, & Driver, 1984; Erickson, 1979, 1985; Stavy & Berkovitz, 1980). This response is likely to be interpreted as an incorrect alternative conception within the specific content area. Erickson (1985), for instance, interpreted these findings in terms of children's conception of temperature. He claimed that children tend to believe that

> temperature is simply a measure of the amount of heat possessed by an object with the operation of mixing together two quantities of water which then leads to a prediction of an overall increase in temperature. (p. 63)

One can, however, interpret this, as well as other responses of this type, from a totally different perspective. It can be argued that these responses evolve from a common source. We have come to call it the intuitive rule "More A–More B". This intuitive rule affects students' responses to comparison tasks regardless of the specific nature of the content domain. That is, we argue that *conceptions, apparently related to specific domains, are actually only specific instances of the use of this rule.*

We were quite surprised to find how widespread the use of this rule is in mathematics and science education. Furthermore, we realized that the same rule is often used in everyday life. Phrases such as "The more you study, the more you know"; "The more money you have, the more you can buy"; and "The more you eat, the stronger you get" occur very regularly in everyday communication. The English language has a special suffix to designate the "more" relation between two quantities, namely, *-er*—as in "the sooner–the better." There is evidence that this rule was applied in ancient times, too: "For in much wisdom is much vexation; And he *that increaseth knowledge increaseth sorrow*" (Ecclesiastes 1:18). Ancient Hebrew, too, manifests the rule: "The *more* possessions, the *more* care . . . the *more* schooling, the *more* wisdom" (Mishna, Nezikim, Aboth, 2.7).

In this chapter of the book we show that the rule "More A–More B" is often used in carrying out comparison tasks. Our main claim is that *this rule is the common core to many reported apparent misconceptions.* We present some examples of the use of this rule in various areas in mathematics and science. We invite you to join us in this venture and encourage you to look for additional examples.

EQUALITY SITUATIONS

The cases in this section involve situations in which two systems differ in one quantity (A) but are equal in another quantity (B). Subjects are asked to compare the two systems with regard to quantity B. The use of the rule "More A–More B" in these cases leads to incorrect responses.

We describe instances of the use of this rule when the equality in quantity B is: (1) directly observable, (2) logically deducible, or (3) scientifically deducible.

Directly Observable Equality

Consider Figure 1.1. When looking at these two lines, one cannot overcome the impression that the lower line segment is longer, although both are of the same length. This well-known optical illusion can be interpreted as an instance of the use of the rule "More A–More B" when A is the length of the whole object in each drawing and B is the length of the line segment only. In spite of the fact that it is possible to directly observe the actual equality in the length of the two line segments, the difference in the total length of the drawings forces us to think that "the longer the object–the longer the line segment." Even after being told that the two line segments are of the same length (or after measuring them), it is next to impossible to overcome this first impression.

The same interpretation could be used to explain the source of students' faulty responses to many other tasks of comparing *perceptually equal quantities*. Here we describe studies concerned with identifying students' conceptions of angle (as an example of a geometrical concept) and of time (a physical concept). Students were presented with two entities that were equal in respect to a directly perceivable quantity, B ($B_1 = B_2$). This equality was not mentioned to the students. The two entities were perceptually different with regard to another quantity, A ($A_1 > A_2$). The students were asked to judge whether B_1 was equal to B_2.

We suggest that in such cases, the difference between A_1 and A_2 might

Figure 1.1. The Two Line Segments Optical Illusion

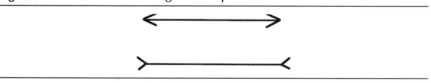

affect students' comparison of B_1 and B_2; that is, they might claim that $B_1 > B_2$ because $A_1 > A_2$ in spite of the observable equality of B_1 and B_2.

Angle. Angle is a main concept in geometry, often defined as the union of two distinct rays that have a common endpoint. Reference to this concept is made from very early on in school (even at the kindergarten level in many countries).

One may therefore ask:

How do people make informal judgments about the equality of angles?

Let us refer to Figure 1.2. In this drawing, two straight lines intersect in point M. The equality of the two vertical angles, α and β, appears to be self-evident. (Of course, from the mathematical point of view, there is a need to prove this.)

Indeed, when this drawing was presented to eighth- and ninth-grade students (aged 14–15), 95% of them argued that the two angles were equal and the level of intuitive acceptance of this judgment was extremely high (Fischbein, Tirosh, & Melamed, 1981). In another study, the very same drawing was presented to students in grades K, 2, 4, 6, and 9. Most students at these grade levels (84%, 78%, 91%, 91%, and 99%, respectively) correctly argued that angles α and β were equal (Tsamir, Tirosh, & Stavy, 1997).

Now let us look at Figure 1.3. As in the previous case, the opposite angles α and β are equal. However, when this drawing was presented to the same group of students in grades K, 2, 4, 6, and 9, the percentages of students who knew that these angles were equal were substantially lower than those in the previous problem (13%, 12%, 62%, 68%, and 82%, respectively). A substantial number of the younger students (grades K, 2, 4, and

Figure 1.2 Vertical Angles—Equal Arms

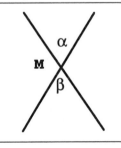

Figure 1.3 Vertical Angles—Unequal Arms

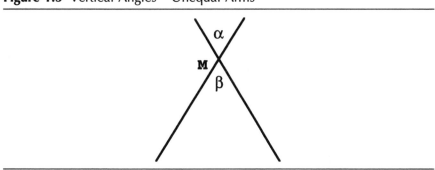

6) argued that angle β was larger. Even some of the older students (grade 9), judged that angle β was larger. This claim was accompanied by the explanation that "angle β is larger because its lines are longer."

> What could be the origin of students' misjudgment when comparing angles α and β?

The immediate, intuitive impression one has when looking at angles α and β is that angle β is larger. One perceptual difference between angles α and β is in the length of their arms. The longer arms of angle β are a basis for the judgment that angle β is larger. This judgment exemplifies the effect of the rule "More A–More B" on students' responses. In this case, the difference between the two angles in quantity A (the perceived length of the arms) affected students' judgment of quantity B (the size of angles α and β).

The perceptual effect of the length of the arms on students' judgments was reported in several other studies investigating the development of students' conception of angle. Foxman and Ruddock (1984) asked pupils to compare angles. They designed items that checked whether pupils compare the actual sizes of the angles involved or other features of the angles that are irrelevant to their size.

One task, presented to 11-year-olds, involved angles drawn on a grid to allow for accurate comparison. The arc length was kept constant; the length of the lines forming the angles was the variable under examination. The drawing, the problem, and the related data are given in Figure 1.4. Angles α and β are actually the same size, but angle β, drawn with a longer arc, was taken to be larger by one-third of the 11-year-olds (grade 5). Similar results were obtained by Tsamir and colleagues (1997).

Figure 1.4 Acute Angles—Unequal Arms

Put a check by the correct answer.

Angle α is bigger than angle β	33%
Angle α is bigger than angle β	4%
Angle α and angle β are the	
Same size	52%
You can't tell	4%
Other	6%

We have so far demonstrated the effect of differences in the length of the arms on students' judgments when comparing angles.

Is the length of the arms the only perceptual factor affecting students' judgments?

Let's look at Figure 1.5. The opposite angles α and β are equal. They are drawn with lines of equal length, but the radius of the arc is deliberately varied.

This drawing was presented to students in grades K, 2, 4, 6, and 9 (the same groups that reacted to Figures 1.2 and 1.3). Here, again, the rate of success in judging equality was relatively low (4%, 11%, 60%, 69%, and 85%, respectively). A substantial number of the students in grades K, 2, 4, and 6 misjudged the equality, claiming that "angle β is bigger than angle α because its arc is longer."

Figure 1.5 Vertical Angles—Unequal Arcs

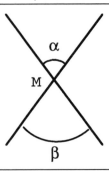

Figure 1.6 Acute Angles—Unequal Arcs

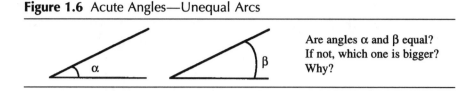

Are angles α and β equal?
If not, which one is bigger?
Why?

The same students were presented with an essentially similar task (Figure 1.6). Again, a non-negligible number of students argued that "angle β is larger because its arc is bigger." Interestingly, some children argued that angle α was larger, a judgment that seems to contradict our claim that students tend to use the intuitive rule "More A–More B" when comparing the size of angles. Yet an examination of students' justifications of their responses shows that the intuitive rule *does* obtain; for instance, "Angle α is larger because the open area in angle α is bigger than the open area in angle β."

Do other factors affect students' judgments when they compare angles?

To investigate this issue, we studied the effect of perceptual differences in the thickness of the arms on students' judgments. Students in grades K, 2, 4, 6, 9 were presented with two equal angles with different arm thicknesses (Figure 1.7). This factor affected young students' judgments in the direction we would expect according to "More A–More B" fallacy.

The three factors discussed so far (length of arms, length of arcs, and thickness of arms) affected students' responses when comparing two equal angles: They reasoned both that "the longer–the larger" and that "the thicker–the larger." This rule was applied most extensively by young students; but even older students, who had studied angles, were affected, although to a lesser extent, by arm length and arc length. The thickness factor affected the responses of young children only.

Figure 1.7 Acute Angles—Unequal Arm Thickness

Responses to the various tasks confirm the pervasive use of the rule "More A–More B." It is noteworthy that the students responded similarly whether the compared angles were vertical or drawn separately.

These perceptual factors affected students' responses in the same direction, yet to different extents. Of the three factors examined in this study, the length of the arms had the most impact, followed by the length of the arcs, with the thickness of the arms being the least influential factor. This seems quite reasonable: The total size of an angle with longer arms is larger than that of the same angle with shorter arms. Similarly, the area bounded by a longer arc is bigger than the area bounded by the same angle with a shorter arc. It is surprising that the thickness of the arms, although it has no bearing on the total size of the drawing, still encourages students to respond with "More A–More B."

We have shown so far that when comparing two equal angles, young children often judge on the basis of perceptual differences rather than the observable equality of the angles. These findings suggest that at a young age differences are more salient to the cognitive system than similarities, thus affecting children's responses to a greater extent. This conclusion is consistent with Vygotsky's (1962) observation that "association by contrast, rather than by similarity, guides the child in compiling a collection" (p. 63).

Although this conclusion holds in general, some perceptual similarities can be salient enough to compete with perceptual differences. A case in point is that of two right angles that differ in the length of their arms, as in Figure 1.8.

Children's responses to problems comparing the sizes of pairs of right angles were somewhat less affected by perceptual differences in arm length than their responses to pairs of acute angles. In everyday life, we come across right angles almost everywhere: wall corners, doors, books, book stands, beds, and so forth. Often, the similarity of right angles is more im-

Figure 1.8 Right Angles—Unequal Arms

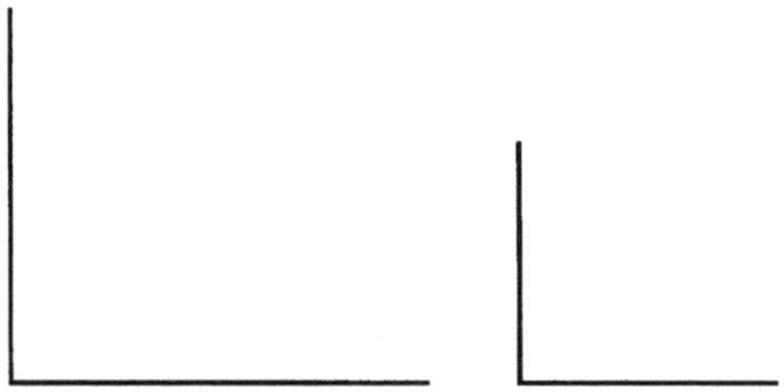

portant in practical situations than the differences involved (e.g., building a tower from bricks, putting a shelf on the wall). Moreover, it has been suggested that vertical and horizontal lines are the basic directions in which objects can be oriented in relation to gravity. The perception of vertical and horizontal lines is, apparently, programmed into the mammalian visual system (Lindsay & Norman, 1972).

The equality in size of right angles was regarded as obvious by Euclid, who included it as a postulate in his famous book, *The Elements*: "All right angles are equal to each other" (in Mueller, 1981, p. 318).

Time. Children's understanding of the concept of time is often analyzed by means of their ability to compare the duration of pairs of events. In a series of studies, Piaget (1969) found that children aged 4 to 9 judged time by the events that occurred during the time span in question. He noted that when two events involve different speeds, the child considers the time span of the faster event to be longer. In the same vein, when two actions conclude with different amounts produced, the child attributes the longer duration to the event that produced the greater amount. In a typical Piagetian experiment, two toy cars ran for the same duration on parallel tracks. Children often claimed that "the car that stopped farther ahead ran for more time" or that "the car that ran faster ran for more time."

In a somewhat different experiment (Piaget, 1969), two figures, one large and one small, were presented to children. The two figures ran a race, starting from a common point A and moving at right angles to each other. In the first stage of the race, the large figure covered a distance of 10 cm while the small one covered a distance of approximately 5 cm over the same duration. In the second stage, the two figures started off from where they had stopped before; now the large figure covered a distance of 20 cm in the same time it took the small one to cover a distance of approximately 10 cm. Finally, in the third stage, the large figure covered a distance of 8 cm while the smaller figure covered a distance of about 4 cm over the same duration. The experimenter's questions aimed to establish whether the subjects recognized the equality of durations in each of the three stages and during the entire race.

Piaget noted that young children (aged 4 to 9) often argued that "the large figure took more time because it went farther." He explained this response with reference to children's conception of time. He argued, for instance, that young children fail to infer the logical relations between the various time concepts of succession, simultaneity, and duration. According to Piaget, only in the concrete operational stage do children come to understand the logical relations between succession and duration, thus becoming able to coordinate time, speed, and distance.

In this experiment, Piaget used comparison tasks in which the objects to be compared were equal in respect to a certain quantity (duration of movement). In all these tasks, the identity of duration could be observed perceptually. However, the bodies involved (cars, figures, etc.) differed in some other perceptual factors (namely, in their speed, the distance they covered, and their size). In fact, Piaget's data show that many of the young children's responses are in line with our suggestion for a general, intuitive rule, "More A–More B" (i.e., "the greater the speed–the more time it takes" and "the greater the distance–the longer the time").

Young children's responses to these tasks are explained by Piaget as follows: When comparing the duration of two events, children often make their judgments according to only one of two equally relevant factors: speed or distance. Because young children are unable to coordinate the various variables involved, they determine time according to only one of them.

According to our thesis concerning the role of the intuitive rule "More A–More B," we may alternatively posit that when young children are asked to compare the duration of two events, they often base their judgments on irrelevant perceptual factors. It is possible to interpret the above results of Piaget's work along these lines. For instance, in the study involving the race, one of the participating figures was larger than the other. This larger figure was also the one that traveled farther. Students' judgments that the larger figure traveled for more time may well have been influenced not only by the observed difference in distance but also by a totally irrelevant factor—namely, the difference in size of the two figures.

Confirmation for this comes from a study of children's conception of time conducted by one of our students (Hakham-Aharon, 1997). She presented children in grades K–6 with two tasks: One tested the effect of the size of a moving object; the other, the effect of the speed/distance traveled. In the first task, the children were first presented with two identical Lego trains. The two trains traveled at the same speed on two parallel tracks. They were connected to the same battery, and the same switch was used to turn both of them on and off. The researcher turned the switch on, and then turned it off when the trains approached the end of the tracks (after traveling about 1 m). The researcher explicitly showed the children that, indeed, the switch controlled both trains. The children were asked whether the trains reached the end of the tracks at the same time and, if not, which arrived first.

All children at all grade levels answered, correctly, that both trains arrived at the same time to the end of the tracks, explaining that "the trains are the same." Then, in front of the children, the researcher rearranged the Lego bricks of one of the trains, making it taller than the other one. Subsequently she asked: "If I now turn on the switch and let the trains travel, will they reach the end of the tracks together?" Clearly, since both trains were controlled by the same switch, the change in the height of one train would affect neither the length of time it moved nor its speed.

A substantial number of participants argued, in line with the intuitive rule "More A–More B," that "the taller train is faster" (40%, 54%, 48%, 34%, and 50% in grades K, 1, 2, 4, and 6, respectively) or "the shorter train is faster" (29%, 23%, 26%, 9%, and 13%). Typical responses were "the taller train travels faster because it is taller/heavier" or "the shorter train travels faster because it is shorter/lighter." Children in the sixth grade invoked such "scientific" factors as air resistance and balance to justify their incorrect judgments; for instance, "The train with the tower is taller, therefore the air hinders its movement."

The second task used a very similar setup. Two identical Lego trains were presented, but each train was controlled by a different switch, with one of the trains traveling faster than the other. Both trains traveled for the same duration of time on two parallel tracks, and thus one came to a halt at a farther point than the other. The researcher made a point of showing that she simultaneously turned the switches of the two trains on and off. Then she asked whether the trains traveled for the same duration of time, and if not, which traveled for more time. In this case, A is the speed/distance traveled of the trains and B is the duration of time they traveled. Almost all children in grades K–4, and 37% of the children in grades 5 and 6 argued, in line with the intuitive rule, that the faster train traveled for a longer duration. Typical responses were "the train that made more way traveled for a longer time because it is farther away" or "the train that moved faster took more time because it passed the other one."

These results show that students' responses to these time-duration tasks were indeed affected not only by the observed difference in distance but also by the differences in size of the two moving objects. Another series of studies, which were concerned with the nature and development of time concept in young children, also confirm that when children are asked to compare two equal durations, they are affected by irrelevant perceptual factors (Levin, 1977, 1979, 1982). In one of these studies, Levin (1982) asked nursery school children and kindergartners to judge whether two lights were lit for the same duration and, if not, which of the two had been on for longer. The lights were switched on for the same duration but differed in size and/ or brightness. Levin's findings indicated that children tended to attribute longer duration significantly more often to the larger than to the smaller light, to the brighter than to the dimmer light, and to the larger and brighter than to the smaller and dimmer light. She concluded that this phenomenon may be based on a mediation mechanism of "any more is more time," which could be regarded as an application of our rule with regard to time.

In this section we described well-known alternative conceptions related to angle and time in the context of the intuitive rule "More A–More B." In the cases of both angle and time, the equality of a pair of presented entities in respect to a certain quantity could be observed with the naked eye. However, as we have shown, various irrelevant perceptual factors affected children's judgments. These included length of angle arms, length of angle arcs, thickness of angle arms, size of moving objects, distance traveled, and size and brightness of lamps.

It has also been shown that the use of the rule "More A–More B" decreases with age and/or instruction. We shall encounter and discuss this phenomenon—the differential effects of various perceptual factors on student responses—in many other instances throughout this book.

Logically Deducible Equality

In the previous section we described well-known alternative conceptions related to angle and time in the context of the intuitive rule "More A–More B." In these cases, although the equality in quantity B could be perceptually observed, students incorrectly claimed that "more A implies more B."

In many comparison situations, however, the equality in quantity B is not directly observable, although it can be logically deduced through the conservation scheme or through the proportion scheme. We shall show that in such situations, students are also affected by the intuitive rule "More A–More B."

Conservation

Let's discuss, for instance, the following task:

> Two identical cups contain equal amounts of water. The water from one of these cups is poured into another cup, which is taller and narrower. Is the amount of water in the first cup equal to the amount of water in the narrower and taller cup? If not, in which cup is there more water? Why?

This is a typical conservation task. Conservation refers to the understanding that quantitative relationships between two objects remain invariant (are conserved) in the face of irrelevant changes. When asked to compare the (equal) amounts of water in the two differently shaped cups, children up to about age 5 or 6 paid attention only to the relative heights of the water in the two cups, arguing that "there is more water in the taller cup" (Piaget, 1952/1965).

This well-known task and other similar ones are often used in an attempt to determine students' understanding of certain concepts (area, weight, volume, etc.). In this type of study, children often argue that "more A (the height of water in the cups) means more B (amount of water)." According to the thesis we suggested previously, such reasoning could be attributed to the application of the intuitive rule "More A–More B."

In these tasks, unlike the ones presented in the previous section, the children were aware of the equality of the two systems in respect to quantity B (amount of water) at the initial stage of the experiment. Yet, unlike in the previous section, after the manipulation, the equality in quantity B could no longer be directly observed; it could, however, be logically derived through the use of the conservation scheme.

In this section we consider students' responses to two types of conservation tasks: conservation of extensive quantities and conservation of intensive quantities. In tasks involving the conservation of extensive quantities, *the identity of the object is usually conserved*. In tasks involving the conservation of intensive quantities, *the identity of the object is usually not conserved*.

Conservation of Extensive Quantities

Extensive quantities are formally defined as follows: If a, b, c, . . . are parts of the system, and y is a property such that $y(\text{system}) = y(a) + y(b) + y(c)$ . . . , then y is said to be an extensive quantity. Properties such as length, weight, area, volume, and energy are extensive quantities.

In a standard conservation task, the participant is first shown two objects that, in addition to being perceptually identical, are known to be equivalent with respect to a certain quantitative property, B. The experimenter then proceeds to deform one of the objects in such a way that its perceptual identity with the first object is lost but its quantitative relationship to quantity B is maintained. This deformation results in a perceptual change in quantity A, which is irrelevant to quantity B. The subject is then asked whether the objects are still equal with respect to quantity B.

Many studies have dealt with students' responses to conservation of specific, extensive quantities. We first examine two classical Piagetian studies and analyze their main findings in light of the suggested intuitive rule "More A–More B."

Number. Piaget (1952/1965) studied children's dependence on length and density when they are asked to compare the number of objects in two rows containing the same number of objects (Figure 1.9). Young children (until about 5 or 6) only paid attention to the relative length of the two rows. Rows of the same length were said to have the same number of objects;

Figure 1.9 Conservation of Number

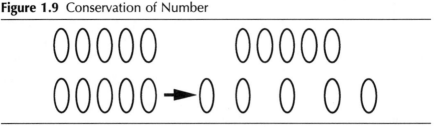

otherwise, *the longer row* was said to be *more numerous* than the shorter row. Some older children based their judgments on the relative density of the two rows, stating that *the denser row* was *more numerous*. These two responses are in line with the intuitive rule "More A (length of row/density of row)–More B (number of objects)."

Area. Piaget, Inhelder, and Szeminska (1960) presented children with two identical rectangular arrangements of six blocks. They then altered one arrangement in the presence of the children by removing two blocks from one end and placing them on the other (Figure 1.10). They then asked the children whether the rectangles were still the same size and still "had the same amount of room." Many children aged 5 to 6 tended to argue that one configuration *was larger* because it *looked longer*. Here, A is the length of the side and B is the area.

When looking at students' responses to these tasks, one might get the impression that the intuitive rule "More A–More B" affects only young

Figure 1.10 Conservation of Area

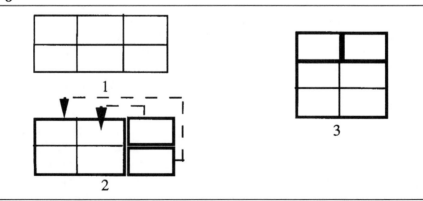

children. However, the following example shows that older students cannot resist this rule either.

Surface area. Livne (1996) presented biology majors in grades 10–12 (ages 16–18) with a task involving conservation of surface area (Figure 1.11). Livne found that only 60%, 58%, and 48% of the biology majors in grades 10, 11, and 12, respectively, conserved the surface area. About a third of the students in each of the grades claimed that the surface area of the unfolded box was larger than that of the folded one. A typical explanation was: "The unfolded box *is longer*; therefore its *surface area is larger*." Others, who claimed that the surface area of the folded box was larger, explained: "The *more folds–the larger the surface*." Clearly, these two types of explanations are instances of the use of the rule "More A (length of box/ number of folds)–More B (surface area)."

Some previous studies, which originally explored children's conceptions of density and state of matter, involved conservation of weight. These studies could be reinterpreted in light of this intuitive rule.

Expansion. Megged (1978) studied children's understanding of the invariance of weight during the process of heating water (Figure 1.12). In this case, the volume of heated water is larger than that of unheated water. The weight, however, remains constant. Many children aged 6 to 10 argued that "the heated water *is heavier* because its volume *is larger*."

Figure 1.11 Conservation of Surface Area

Two opposite faces of a rectangular-shaped box A were folded in the way described in the following drawing:

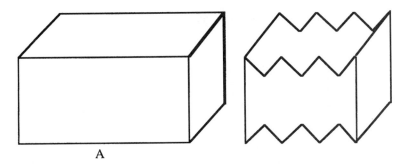

A

Is the surface area of the unfolded box larger than/smaller than/equal to the surface area of the folded box? Explain your choice.

Figure 1.12 Expansion: Conservation of Weight

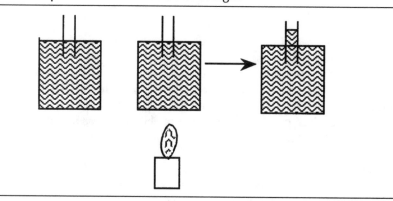

Change of state. Stavy and Stachel (1985) studied children's conceptions of solid and liquid. They presented children aged 5 to 15 with two identical candles, one of which was then melted (Figure 1.13). The child was asked about the equality of weight (whether the solid candle and the melted one weighed the same). Many children between ages 6 and 10 argued that "the solid candle is *harder or stronger* than the liquid candle and therefore it *weighs more.*"

In all the above conservation tasks and in many other similar ones, the manipulation of one of the objects consisted of deforming its shape, location, or state. In these transformations, the object before and after the manipulation remained the same—no part of the object was removed, and nothing was added to it. It would be interesting to find out whether in other essen-

Figure 1.13 Melting: Conservation of Weight

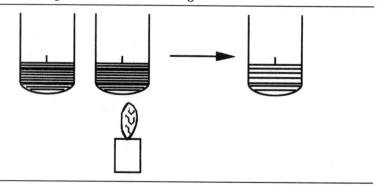

tially similar tasks, when the identity of the object before and after the manipulation is not maintained, the intuitive rule would be even more dominant than in cases where the identity of the object is maintained.

Perimeter. We designed a plastic polygon to test for conservation of perimeter (Figure 1.14). In this task, the identity of the object was not conserved, since part of the rectangle was removed, yet the perimeter remained the same.

Azhari (1998) presented children in grades 1, 3, 5, 7, and 9 with this task. She found that at all these grade levels, including the higher ones, at least 70% of the respondents claimed incorrectly that the perimeter of the rectangle was larger than that of the polygon because "the rectangle is larger," "the rectangle has more area," "a corner was not taken away," and so forth. These high percentages of "More A (area, or size of rectangle)–More B (size of perimeter)" suggest that (1) when the identity of the object is not conserved, responses are very strongly affected by the intuitive rule "More A–More B," and (2) this effect does not decrease with age. To further confirm our hypothesis that the effect of the intuitive rule "More A–More B" becomes more overriding when the identity of the object is not conserved, Azhari presented the oldest participants (grade 9) with a thread polygon task (Figure 1.15).

Figure 1.14 Plastic Polygon

Two identical plastic rectangles are presented, each consisting of a small square at the upper right corner and a polygon. The small square is removed from the upper right corner of one of the rectangles. A polygon is obtained.

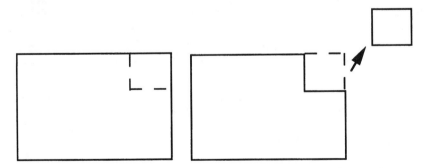

Is the perimeter of the obtained polygon equal to/not equal to the perimeter of the original rectangle?
If equal, explain why. If not equal, which is bigger? Why?

Figure 1.15 Thread Polygon

Two identical rectangles are made by means of two identical threads on a nail board. The thread that formed one of the rectangles was removed from the upper right corner of the rectangle and rearranged, creating a polygon.

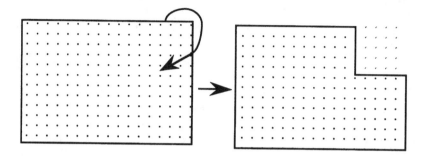

Is the perimeter of the obtained polygon equal to/not equal to the perimeter of the original rectangle?
If equal, explain why. If not equal, which is bigger? Why?

Azhari found that 45% of the students incorrectly argued, in line with the intuitive rule, that the perimeter of the rectangle was larger than that of the polygon. This percentage is lower than that given by students in the same grade level to the previous, essentially similar task (70%).

The difference in responses to these two essentially similar tasks indicates that the use of the intuitive rule is somewhat affected by the specific information given in each situation. It seems that removing part of the object (the small rectangle) supports the use of the rule "More A–More B," because it emphasizes difference, while the fact that the object is conserved (same thread) emphasizes the equality. These data also indicate that at least a quarter of the ninth-graders who participated in this study gave contradictory answers to essentially the same comparison-of-perimeter task. This casts doubt on the interpretation of responses to tasks involving comparison of perimeter in terms of alternative conceptions of perimeter.

Azhari presented these two tasks (the plastic polygon and the thread polygon) only to one age group of students. She carried out her study among a Hebrew-speaking population in Israel. A larger-scale study addressing essentially the same issue (i.e., the effect of identity of the object on the extent to which students apply the intuitive rule "More A–More B") was carried out by Zahir (1997). This study was carried out among an Arabic-speaking population in Israel. He presented students in grades 5, 7, 9, and 11 with two tasks (Figure 1.16 and Figure 1.17).

In each of these tasks, the perimeters of the involved objects before and after the change were the same, while the areas were not. Thus, in both these tasks the change is not relevant to the perimeter. The two tasks, however, differed in respect to the identity of involved objects: In the thread-rectangle task the identity of the objects creating the perimeters (i.e., the threads) was conserved, while in the adding-a-square task the identity of the objects was not conserved because a square was added to one of the polygons.

There were substantial differences in students' responses to these two

Figure 1.16 Thread Rectangle

Compare the area and the perimeter of two identical closed threads with the same circular shape.
Change the shape of each thread to achieve two different-shaped rectangles:

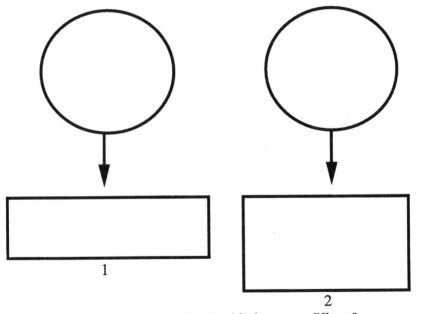

Are the perimeters of the two rectangles (1 and 2) the same or different?
If different, which is larger? Why?
Are the areas bounded by the threads (1 and 2) the same or different?
If different, which is larger? Why?

Figure 1.17 Adding a Square

Compare the area and the perimeter of the two polygons, each composed of eight equal squares. Add one square to one of the polygons in the following way:

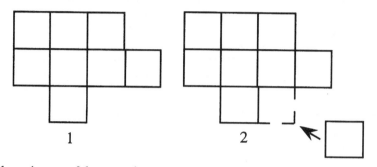

1   2

Are the perimeters of the two polygons (1 and 2) the same or different?
If different, which is larger? Why?
Are the areas of the two polygons (1 and 2) the same or different?
If different, which is larger? Why?

tasks. The percentages of students who correctly claimed that the perimeters before and after the change were equal were much lower in the second task than in the first one (5%, 9%, 10%, 20% versus 38%, 43%, 79%, and 70% in grades 5, 7, 9 and 11, respectively). Adding a square to the object in the second task seems to have emphasized the perceptual differences between the objects and thus to have encouraged the application of the rule "More A (an additional square)–More B (length of perimeter)."

In this section, we have shown that many students at different age levels are affected to different extents by the intuitive rule "More A–More B" when responding to a variety of tasks involving conservation of extensive quantities. A similar phenomenon was observed with tasks related to intensive quantities.

CONSERVATION OF INTENSIVE QUANTITIES

Intensive quantities are defined as follows: "If a, b, c, . . . are parts of a system, and y is a property such that $y(a) = y(b) = y(c) . . .$, then y is said to be an intensive quantity. The value of y for the entire system may be defined by $y(\text{system}) = y(\text{any part})$. Clearly y(system) is independent of the size (or extent) of the system" (Canagaratna, 1992, p. 957).

Tasks involving intensive quantities consist of presenting the subject with two systems that are identical with respect to a certain intensive quantity but that differ in size. The subject is asked to judge or to compare the values of the intensive quantity in the two systems.

Concentration. Stavy, Strauss, Orpaz, and Carmi (1982) presented children with three cups of sugarwater of the same concentration. The contents of two of these cups were poured into an empty cup, and the children were asked to estimate the sweetness (concentration) of the combined water compared to that of the water in the original third cup (Figure 1.18).

It was found that the majority of children aged 6 to 10 claimed that the combined water was sweeter. Two types of justifications were presented—"the one with more sugar is sweeter" and "the one with more water is sweeter." Both of these justifications share the structure of "More A (water, sugar)–More B (sweetness)." In this case, the perceptual difference in the quantity of water was salient and directly elicited "the more water–the sweeter" response. Most likely, this salient difference in the amount of water also indirectly encouraged "the more sugar–the sweeter" response. The reasoning behind this response was probably that "more water–more sugar" and therefore "more sugar–sweeter."

Temperature. Strauss, Stavy, and Orpaz (1977) presented children with three cups containing equal amounts of equally hot water. The water from two of the cups was poured into an empty cup, and children were asked to compare the "hotness" of the water in the combined cup with that of the third cup's contents (Figure 1.19).

The majority of children aged 6 to 8 claimed that the water in the combined cup was hotter. These incorrect judgments were justified with reference to the amount of water, namely, "the more water–the warmer."

Figure 1.18 Conservation of Concentration

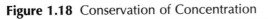

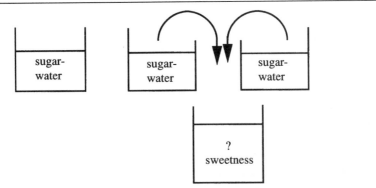

Figure 1.19 Conservation of Temperature

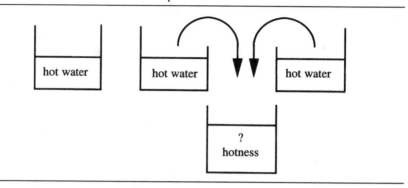

A similar response was observed with older students who were presented with the same problem and also given numerical temperature values (e.g., 40°C in each cup). Most children aged 7 to 11 argued that the temperature of the combined water was higher than that in the original cup. These responses were often accompanied by an arithmetic calculation (e.g., 40°C + 40°C = 80°C).

Proportion

The concept of proportion is widely used in mathematics, science, and everyday life. Proportion could be defined as an equality of two ratios, namely, $\frac{a}{b} = \frac{c}{d}$. The development of proportional reasoning was extensively studied by Piaget and his collaborators (Inhelder & Piaget, 1958; Piaget, Grize, Szeminska, & Bang, 1968) as well as many others. Typical proportion problems that have been used in these studies are comparison problems of the following type: "Car A is driven 180 km in 2 hours. Car B is driven 270 km in 3 hours. Which car drove faster, or were their speeds equal?" The equality in the speed in this problem is deduced by using the proportional scheme $\left[\frac{180}{2} = \frac{270}{3}\right]$.

Research has shown that many students were impressed by the magnitudes of the two extensive quantities (distance and time) and concluded that car B drove faster because "it covered a larger distance" and/or "it drove for more time." Obviously, such responses could evolve from an application of the intuitive rule "More A (distance, time)–More B (speed)."

Many common responses to various tasks involving proportional reasoning could be reinterpreted in light of the intuitive rule "More A–More

B." Here we examine the rule as it relates to fractions, probability, and concentration.

Fractions. Research related to comparison of fractions has revealed that when students in middle school are asked to compare two equal fractions, they often conclude that one of them is larger because "its top and bottom numbers are larger," for example, "$\frac{4}{6}$ is bigger than $\frac{2}{3}$ because 4 is larger than 2 and 6 is larger than 3" (see, e.g., Hart et al., 1980).

Similar responses have been observed, in much higher grades, with algebraic fractions. Rapaport (1998) presented high school students with the following tasks:

Mark >, =, <, or "impossible to determine":

1. $\dfrac{16y}{8} \,\square\, 2y$

2. $\dfrac{2a - 8}{2} \,\square\, \dfrac{6a - 24}{6}$

These two tasks are essentially similar: Each presents two equivalent algebraic expressions. The differences in the percentages of correct responses to these two tasks are striking. While the vast majority of students at all grade levels correctly answered the first question, only about half (or less) did so with regard to the second problem. Clearly, the equality of the two algebraic fractions in the second problem is less obvious than in the first one. In the first expression, it is enough to recognize the equality of $\frac{16}{8}$ and 2 in order to provide a correct response. However, in the second task, recognizing the equality demands several operations. In such cases, where mental demands are higher, students are primarily affected by the salient differences between the two expressions (different numbers) and are thus less resistant to the effect of the intuitive rule. Consequently, they argue, incorrectly, that " $\frac{6a-24}{6}$ is bigger because all numbers in this expression are larger."

Probability. In a large survey of adolescents' concepts of probability (Green, 1983), subjects were presented with a typical probability problem (Figure 1.20). About half the students in this study incorrectly chose bag K as more likely to yield a black counter, most of them reasoning that "there are more black ones in bag K."

Figure 1.20 Probability
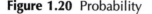

Two bags have black and white counters.
Bag J: 3 black and 1 white.
Bag K: 6 black and 2 white.
Which bag gives a better chance of picking a *black* counter?

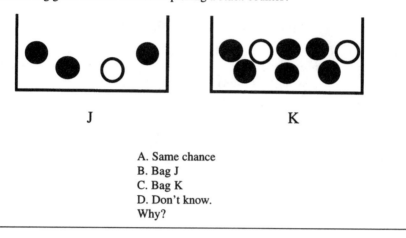

A. Same chance
B. Bag J
C. Bag K
D. Don't know.
Why?

Concentration. Stavy and colleagues (1982) presented children with two cups of sugarwater of the same concentration. One cup was filled with water and 2 teaspoons of sugar were added and mixed in. The other cup was half-full of water and 1 teaspoon of sugar was added and mixed in. The children were asked whether the taste of the sugarwater in both cups would be the same or different and, if it would be different, in which cup they would expect the sugarwater to be sweeter (Figure 1.21). The majority of the children aged 5 to 8 claimed that "the cup with more sugar would be sweeter" or that "the cup with more water would be sweeter" or that "the cup with more water and more sugar would be sweeter."

Figure 1.21 Concentration: Proportion

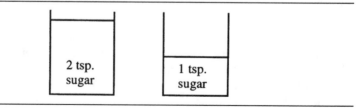

In the cases included in this section, the equality could be deduced by the logical schemes of conservation or proportion. However, many students' incorrect responses to these tasks share the structure "More A–More B." We have shown that the identity of the object somewhat suppresses the effect of the rule. In respect to proportion, the use of the rule could be elicited by relating either to the numerator (e.g., the "top number" of the fraction, number of white counters, amount of sugar) or to the denominator (the "bottom number" of the fraction, number of black counters, volume of water) or to both, since both changed in the same direction. Interestingly, it seems that the intuitive rule could be activated not only by obvious perceptual differences but also by salient differences between symbols associated with perceptual images (e.g., numbers).

Scientifically Deducible Equality

"I see it, but I don't believe it" (Cantor, in a letter to Dedekind, June 29, 1887)

Infinite sets. If you ask students and adults to respond to the problem presented in Figure 1.22, you will realize that many claim with great confidence that "line segment CD contains more points than line segment AB because it contains all points in line segment AB and additional ones." Others, however, will argue without hesitation that "both line segments have the same number of points, that is, infinity."

Each of these contradictory answers seems reasonable. How can we find out which is the right one? In the history of mathematics, you will find echoes of this dilemma in Galileo's writings. The following excerpt is taken from Galileo's *Dialogues Concerning Two New Sciences*. This dialogue is between Simplicio, the simple man, and Salviati, representing Galileo:

Figure 1.22 Points in Different-Length Line Segments

Consider the following two line segments:

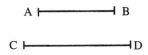

In your opinion, is the number of points in line segment CD smaller than/equal to/larger than the number of points in line segment AB?
Explain your answer.

Simplicio: Here a difficulty presents itself which appears to me insoluble. Since it is clear that we may have one line greater than another, each containing an infinite number of points, we are forced to admit that, within one and the same class we may have something greater than infinity, because the infinity of points in the long line is greater than the infinity of points in the short line. This assigning to an infinite quantity a value greater than infinity is quite beyond my comprehension.

Salviati: This is one of the difficulties which arises when we attempt, with our finite minds, to discuss the infinite, assigning to it those properties which we give to the finite and limited: but this I think is wrong, for we cannot speak of infinite quantities as being the one greater or less than or equal to another . . . and finally the attributes "equal," "greater," and "less," are not applicable to infinite, but only to finite quantities. (Galileo, 1638/1954, p. 31)

Galileo concluded that infinite quantities are incomparable. This conclusion, formulated in Aristotle's time (384–322 B.C.), held for centuries. Cantor, at the end of the nineteenth century, presented an entirely different approach to this issue. He defined the term *equal* in the following manner: Two sets are considered to have the same cardinal number if they can be put into a 1–1 correspondence with each other. This definition applies for both finite and infinite sets.

Let's now return to our original question, namely, how can one find out if the number of points in line segment CD is smaller than/equal to/larger than the number of points in line segment AB. The equality of the number of points in the two different-length line segments is a direct consequence of Cantor's above-mentioned definition. The 1–1 correspondence between the points on these line segments is formed by drawing the lines CAO and DBO, considering the beam of rays from O to the line segments, and then pairing each point on CD with the corresponding point (i.e., the point on the same ray) on AB (Figure 1.23). Someone who is unfamiliar with the Cantorian definition of equivalent sets will either be affected by the fact that one line segment is longer than the other, hence arguing that there are more points in the longer line segment, or will claim that each line segment contains an infinite number of points, hence arguing that it is impossible to compare them (Tirosh, 1985). This illustrates that a person who is unfamiliar with the relevant formal definition of equivalence of infinite sets will most likely be impressed by irrelevant perceptual information and consequently respond in line with the intuitive rule. Here we describe other similar cases from other scientific domains.

Figure 1.23 One-to-One Correspondence Between Points on Line Segments

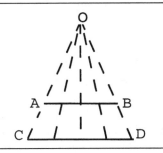

We interpret two cases, previously discussed within the alternative-conception paradigm, in light of the intuitive rule "More A–More B." Then we describe a newly designed task aimed at testing the predictive power of this intuitive rule.

Free-fall. Let us think about the question presented in Figure 1.24. Children and many adults claim that the full matchbox will hit the ground first. However, when the experiment is carried out, it is obvious that the boxes reach the ground at the same time. The physical explanation of these results is rooted in Newtonian mechanics. The potential energy of the empty matchbox is defined as PE = mgh (when m is the mass of the empty match-

Figure 1.24 Free-Fall

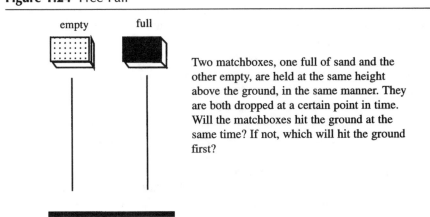

Two matchboxes, one full of sand and the other empty, are held at the same height above the ground, in the same manner. They are both dropped at a certain point in time. Will the matchboxes hit the ground at the same time? If not, which will hit the ground first?

box, g is the acceleration of gravity, and h is the height of the body above ground). As the body falls, its potential energy (PE) is transformed into kinetic energy (KE), defined as $KE = \frac{1}{2}mv^2$ (v is the speed of the empty matchbox when it reaches the ground). According to the law of conservation of energy, $PE = KE$, namely $mgh = \frac{1}{2}mv^2$. Consequently, $gh = \frac{1}{2}v^2$ and $v = \sqrt{2gh}$. This shows that the speed of the falling body depends on the height from which it falls; it is independent of the mass of the body. Therefore the two matchboxes will reach the ground at the same time.

Why do children and adults argue that the full matchbox will reach the ground first? It is our belief that the subjects are influenced by the (irrelevant) weight difference of the two matchboxes and claim, in line with the intuitive rule "More A–More B", that "the heavier–the faster." Similar tasks were presented to various groups of students, including first-year college physics students, and similar reactions were reported (Champagne, Klopfer, & Anderson, 1979; Gunstone & White, 1981).

Here, too, the history of science reflects the natural tendency to apply the rule "More A–More B" when adequate scientific knowledge is not available. The notion that the speed of a free-falling object depends on its weight was widely accepted in the ancient world. Aristotle, for example, thought an object's falling time was proportionally related to its weight; that is, if an object is twice the weight of another object, it will move twice as rapidly as the other. Philiponus, who lived in the sixth century, doubted Aristotle's assertion regarding the proportional relationship between the weight and the speed of falling bodies, but he still could not give up the idea that "the heavier–the faster." He suggested that the falling time of a heavier object was somewhat shorter than that of a lighter object. The first to indicate that the falling time of an object is independent of its weight was Galileo, in the sixteenth century. He based his claim on experimental evidence and on thought experiments. Later on, Newton provided a coherent, formal explanation for this observation.

Time and distance. The problem described in Figure 1.25 is often introduced to students of physics. The correct answer to this question is that the crossing times of the boat on the first and second days are equal. This derives from the principle of independence of motions; that is, when a body moves under the influence of a number of motions, it is possible to consider each of these motions separately and independently from the others, so that any change in one of the motions does not affect the others.

When this problem was presented to high school students, many chose the first statement, arguing that the longer the distance the boat traveled, the

Figure 1.25 Crossing Time and Distance

A motorboat crosses a river, from point A to point B. Its engine speed is constant, and the direction of its wheel is perpendicular to the riverbanks.
1. One morning the boat left from point A and arrived at point B. On this day, the river was quiet, without any current whatsoever.
2. On another morning, the same boat, again, was meant to cross the river from point A to point B. This time, however, a strong current swept the boat away, and it arrived at point C.

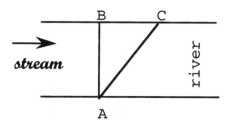

Choose the right answer, and explain your choice:
1. The crossing time on the first day was smaller than that on the second day.
2. The crossing time on the second day was smaller than that on the first day.
3. The crossing time on the first and second days were equal.

more time it took to cross the river (Morabia, 1990). We presented this problem to students in grades 7 to 12. At each grade level, more than 50% of the students incorrectly claimed, in line with the rule "More A (distance between endpoints)–More B (duration of time)," that the crossing on the first day took less time than on the second day. About 30% of the seventh-graders argued that on the second day the boat travels faster but goes a longer distance—and therefore its traveling time is the same. The highest percentage of correct responses accompanied by correct justifications (37%) was provided by tenth-graders, probably due to related instruction. Interestingly, this percentage dropped in higher grades, where most students responded, again, in line with the intuitive rule.

Cell size. Consider the following two tasks:

Is the size of a muscle cell of a mouse bigger than/equal to/ smaller than a muscle cell of an elephant? Explain your choice.

A kitten grows into an adult cat. Is a liver cell of a kitten bigger than/equal to/smaller than a liver cell of a grown-up cat? Explain your choice.

The correct answer to both these tasks is "equal to." In fact, "most cells of most organisms from minuscule nematode worms to enormous whales are roughly 10 micrometers in diameter" (McMahon & Bonner, 1983, pp. 7–8). The scientific explanation of this surprising phenomenon refers to the relationship between the surface area and volume of the cell. Munro, for instance, explained that:

> At the cellular level the oxygen vital for aerobic metabolism moves by diffusion. There is no molecular pump that can speed the movement of the oxygen across the cell membrane. . . . The removal of the waste product is similarly dependent upon diffusion. . . . If there were an evolution of geometrically similar but larger cell, say by doubling the diameter . . . the rate of diffusion will be doubled. But meanwhile the volume of the cell would have increased as the cube of linear dimension 2^3. Thus it was not practical to remain unicellular in the evolution of the body size. . . . This confirmed that "the larger mammals have more cells, not larger cells." (Munro, 1969, quoted in Calder, 1996, pp. 357–358)

We predicted that students would tend to argue, in line with the intuitive rule "More A–More B," that the cells of the larger animal are larger. To test this hypothesis, a questionnaire including these two tasks was submitted to seventh- to twelfth-grade students.

Our data show that the majority of the students (especially in grades 7 and 8) incorrectly claimed that larger animals have larger cells. Common justifications for this judgment, at all grade levels, were: "According to the dimensions of elephants and those of mice, it is obvious that the muscle cells of mice are smaller than those of elephants"; "The mouse is smaller than the elephant"; "The kitten cells grow as it grows"; and "The liver of the kitten grows and consequently its cells have to grow."

Most of the younger students who correctly claimed that the cells are of equal sized attributed this equality to the fact that the cells have the same function. Most of those at the upper grade levels who provided correct responses relied on their formal, biological knowledge about cells. Typical responses were: "The size of the cell is independent of the size of the animal"; "A cell is a cell and the type of the animal does not make a difference"; and "All the cells are of the same size, but elephants/cats have more cells."

In this section we described several comparison tasks, taken from different scientific domains. Students were asked to determine whether two systems were equal in a certain quantity. In all these cases, the systems were equal with regard to the related quantity, but this equality could be neither perceptually observed nor logically derived. The equality could, however, be scientifically deduced. In all these tasks, many students were prompted by perceptual differences in an irrelevant quantity to argue that "More A–More B."

INEQUALITY SITUATIONS

In the previous section we presented numerous examples of comparison situations in which many students worked in accordance with the rule "More A–More B." In all these cases, the application of this rule led them astray: They concluded that more A implies more B. In all these situations this conclusion was erroneous because the two systems were equal with respect to quantity B.

In this chapter we examine two other types of comparison situations in which the application of the rule "More A–More B" leads to incorrect judgments:

1. Quantities A and B are in inverse ratio; that is, when A increases, B proportionally decreases.
2. The relations between A and B are not fixed. This happens when B increases proportionally with A for certain intervals but not for others, or when there is no fixed relationship between A and B.

Inverse Ratio Between A and B

Consider the following two tasks:

1. Is $\frac{1}{2}$ smaller than/equal to/larger than $\frac{1}{3}$?
2. Is 0.1 smaller than/equal to/larger than 0.01?

Clearly, in both cases, the first fraction is larger than the second one. However, young children tend to argue that the second fraction is larger: "3 is larger than 2; therefore 1/3 is larger than 1/2" (e.g., Pitkethly & Hunting, 1996) or, similarly, "hundreds are bigger than tens, therefore 0.01 is larger than 0.1" (Nesher, 1986). Obviously, these responses are in line with the intuitive rule "More A–More B."

Let's look at another pair of tasks (Figures 1.26 and 1.27). Studies exploring students' responses to these tasks reported that some young children (aged 4 to 8) claimed that "the more water–the sweeter" and "the more

Figure 1.26 Concentration: Inverse Ratio

Consider the following two sugar solutions:
-Solution I was prepared by mixing 1 teaspoon of sugar into 1 cup of water.
-Solution II was prepared by mixing the same-sized teaspoon of sugar into half a cup of water:

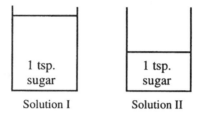

Is the sweetness of these two solutions the same or different? If different, in which cup is the sugarwater sweeter?

water – the cooler" (e.g., Stavy, 1981). A more frequent response in these cases, however, is "the same (amount of sugar/number of ice cubes)–the same (sweetness/temperature)." Such "same–same" responses are discussed in Chapter 2.

These four tasks are often referred to as "inverse-ratio tasks." In such tasks, students are asked to compare two ratios (e.g., fractions, concentrations, or temperatures). The numerators in each task are the same, while the denominators are different. In all these cases, some young children who had not yet acquired the proportion scheme incorrectly claimed that "the larger the denominator–the larger the ratio."

The application of the intuitive rule "More A–More B" is manifested to a larger extent in the first two tasks. A possible explanation of this difference in the application of the rule is that in the first two tasks the differences in the denominators are very salient, making the "equal" answer seem impossible. Therefore, children who have not yet acquired the proportion scheme can hardly claim anything other than that $\frac{1}{3} > \frac{1}{2}$. However, in the concentration and temperature tasks, the similarity between the numerators (1 teaspoon of sugar, 1 ice cube) is associated with the quantity children are asked about (sweetness and temperature). Consequently, many students argue, incorrectly, for equality. The same behavior (responses of the type "larger denominator–larger ratio") was reported by researchers who studied the development of logical schemes (i.e., Karplus, Karplus, Formisano, & Paulsen, 1977; Noelting, 1980a, 1980b; Shayer & Adey, 1981; Strauss & Stavy, 1982).

Figure 1.27 Temperature: Inverse Ratio

Take two identical containers. From the same jug, pour a cup of water into one container and a half a cup into the other container.
Add one ice cube to each of the containers. Let the water cool for a while.

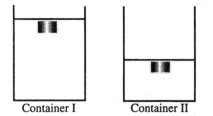

Container I   Container II

Is the temperature in containers 1 and 2 the same or different? If different, in which container is the water cooler?

The Relationship Between A and B Is Not Fixed

Let's look at the graph in Figure 1.28. This graph describes phenomena in various scientific domains, including the rise in temperature of a substance with energy input (physics), growth curves of populations (biology and sociology), and velocity of enzymatic reaction with concentration of substrate (biochemistry), just to mention a few. Section I in this graph "behaves" in accordance with the intuitive rule "More A–More B." The behavior of the graph in section II changes as B becomes constant.

Figure 1.28 Different Relationships Between A and B

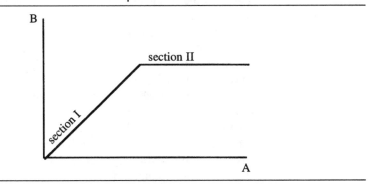

Let's now turn to one specific example—that of the rise of temperature with energy input. When water is heated at a constant rate, its temperature increases linearly until the water starts boiling (at 100°C). The temperature of the water stays constant when the heating continues. The heat energy supplied to the water converts the water from liquid to gas. Only later on, when all water is transformed into gas, will the temperature of the gaseous water start rising again.

In your opinion, how would students react to the following task involving temperature and boiling:

> A saucepan of water with a thermometer in it is placed on a hot-plate set on high. After 5 minutes, the water starts boiling. The thermometer then registers 100°C. The water continues boiling with the hot-plate on high. What does the thermometer register after 5 minutes of boiling? Mark with X.
> _____ more than 100°C
> _____ 100°C
> _____ less than 100°C
> *Please explain your thinking!*

You would probably assume that children would argue that the temperature of the water 5 minutes after the onset of boiling would be higher than 100°C, explaining that "the longer you heat–the higher the temperature."

Indeed, several studies conducted in different countries confirmed this hypothesis (e.g., Avrams, 1989; Linn, Layman, & Nachmias, 1987). Andersson (1979), for instance, reported that 40%, 24%, 13%, and 16% of Swedish students in grades 6, 7, 8, and 9, respectively, gave such a response to this question.

Children know from their daily experience that the temperature of an object rises when heated (i.e., "the more you heat–the warmer it gets"). This experience is consistent with the intuitive rule "More A–More B." The first part of the graph in Figure 1.28 describes this linear relationship. Children assume that this relationship between duration of heating and temperature will continue, namely, that "the more you heat–the higher the temperature." There is no reason for them to assume that the relationship breaks down at a certain point. In fact, only formal knowledge related to heat, temperature, and change in the state of matter would lead to a correct response and compete with the intuitive rule "More A–More B."

Similar findings were reported by Zohar (1995) in her study of reasoning about interactions between variables. In this study, she asked community college students to solve problems involving microworlds. One of these microworlds consisted of a set of manipulative features that influence the speed of model boats. Students were asked to explore the effects of various variables (boat size, sail size, sail color, depth of water, and presence or absence of weight) on the speed of the boat. Zohar was mainly interested in investigating students' ability to determine the interaction between two of these variables: boat size and presence or absence of weight. In this specific microworld, presence of weight had no effect on the speed of the large boat. Yet in the case of the small boat, the presence of weight lowered the speed. Zohar reported that one participant's initial theory, as assessed before she started experimenting with the task, was that weight makes a difference: It slows boats down. This subject started experimenting with the large boat and realized that "the weight did not make a difference." Yet after experimenting with the small boat, she concluded that "the more the weight–the slower it goes," making no reference to her initial observation of the large boat. Zohar explained that "the student ignored her first inference about weight in a large boat, which contradicted her initial theory, and stated only her second conclusion about weight in a small boat, which confirmed this theory" (p. 1052). The student continued experimenting, commenting that "the weight makes a difference: The lighter, the faster" (p. 1053). Only after 24 experiments did the student made the valid interaction inference, namely, that "in the small boat, the weight makes a difference, but it does not in the large boat" (p. 1053).

In light of the intuitive rule "More A–More B," we interpret this behavior as follows: The task is a comparison task, involving two properties—weight and speed of boat. According to the intuitive rule, students argue that "the larger the weight, the slower it goes." Indeed, this was the student's initial response (before experimenting). The fact that she maintained "the heavier–the slower" for 24 trials, although she faced contradictory evidence, exemplifies the profound effect of the intuitive rule.

In mathematics, some properties often hold for certain number systems but break down when the realm of numbers is extended. For instance, when comparing two natural numbers by means of the number line, one could argue that the number that is farther from zero is the larger number (the farther–the larger). When applied to real numbers, however, this rule may incorrectly lead to, for instance, a statement that −5 is larger than −2 because "it is farther from zero." The rule "the farther–the larger" holds for all natural numbers but not for all real ones. The same incorrect conclusion is also reached by students when they disregard the role of the minus sign, referring only to the absolute value of the number.

In general, when two natural numbers—n and $n + a$ (a is also a natural number)—are compared, students, from relatively early on, know that $n + a > n$. Many studies in mathematics education report that when asked to compare pairs of numerical or algebraic expressions (e.g., negative numbers, powers, multiplication expressions involving variables, trigonometric expressions), students often incorrectly apply their knowledge of natural numbers (see, e.g., Bell, 1982; Fischbein, 1987; Hart, 1981).

In line with the intuitive rule "More A–More B," such incorrect responses could be explained in the following manner: When asked to compare two expressions, for instance, 4x and 2x, that differ in a salient quantity A ($A_1 > A_2$, that is, $4 > 2$), students deduced that $B_1 > B_2$ (namely $4x > 2x$). In the same vein, they argue, when comparing two expressions involving n and $n + a$, that $-(n + a) > -n$, $x(n + a) > xn$, $(n + a)^x > n^x$, $x^{(n+a)} > x^n$, and so forth. In all these examples, the two expressions to be compared differ in a salient quantity ($n + a > n$). The students "deduced" that since $n + a$ is greater than n, the direction of the inequality between the entire expressions, B_1 and B_2, will be preserved.

Some of our collaborators have designed specific tasks to examine the role of the intuitive rule "More A–More B" in students' responses to comparison tasks involving mathematical expressions (Kopelevich, 1997; Rapaport, 1998; Shohet, 1994; Zagury, 1997). Here we report only on some of their findings.

Rapaport (1998) presented students in grades 9 to 12 with comparison tasks of algebraic expressions. Three such tasks were as follows:

Mark <, =, >, or "impossible to determine":
1. $4x \ \square \ 2x$
2. $3 (a + b) \ \square \ 2 (a + b)$
3. $\dfrac{3x}{2} \ \square \ \dfrac{5x}{2}$

Table 1.1 shows that the vast majority of the students at each of these grade levels gave incorrect answers to these problems. These responses are in line with the rule "More A–More B." Common justifications were: "4 is larger than 2; therefore 4x is larger than 2x"; "3 is larger than 2; therefore $3 (a + b) > 2 (a + b)$"; "5 is greater than 3; therefore $\frac{5x}{2}$ is greater than $\frac{3x}{2}$; "I reduced the x, and compared the numbers."

Kopelevich (1997) asked students in grades 7, 9, 10, and 11 to compare expressions involving powers. Two of her tasks were as follows:

1. Rami claimed that if t is larger than m ($t > m$), then $a^t > a^m$. Is Rami right? Yes/no.
2. Dana claimed that if a is larger than b ($a > b$), then $a^t > b^t$. Is she right? Yes/no.

Table 1.1 Distribution, by Grade, of "More A –More B" Incorrect Responses to Comparison of Algebraic Expressions (in %)

	Grade			
	9	10	11	12
n =	(68)	(68)	(66)	(63)
4x > 2x	90	84	66	69
3(a + b) > 2(a + b)	91	95	69	57
$\frac{5x}{2} > \frac{3x}{2}$	86	85	73	57

At least 50% of the students at each of these grade levels incorrectly agreed with each of these statements, claiming that if t > m, then $a^t > a^m$ and that if a > b, then $a^t > b^t$. When asked to put the correct symbol (>, =, <, or [impossible to determine]) between the expressions a^3 and a^4, more than 65% of the students at each of these grade levels argued that a^4 is greater than a^3 because "it has a larger power."

In both these studies (Kopelevich, 1997; Rapaport, 1998), the percentages of incorrect judgments in accordance with the rule "More A–More B" are extremely high. The strong activation of the rule in each of these tasks is probably a result of the differences between the numbers on the different sides of the mathematical expressions.

SOME QUESTIONS ABOUT THE USE OF THIS RULE

In the previous two sections, we explored many content domains in both mathematics and science: arithmetic, geometry, algebra, probability, infinity, mechanics, thermodynamics, chemistry, and biology. One would assume that students' responses to tasks vary with the specific domain and reflect alternative conceptions related to these content domains. There is no reason to assume that the same pattern of responses will occur in relation to questions in these different domains. However, we have shown that students supplied "More A–More B" responses to the various tasks presented in these sections.

How Can This Surprising Behavior Be Explained?

All the tasks described in this chapter are comparison tasks. In each of them, the student is asked to compare two objects (or two systems) that differ in a certain salient quantity, A ($A_1 > A_2$). The student is asked to compare the two objects or systems with respect to another quantity, B, where B_1 is not greater than B_2 (that is, $B_1 = B_2$ or $B_1 < B_2$). In several cases we have shown that while some students judged, in line with the intuitive rule, that $B_1 > B_2$ because $A_1 > A_2$, some others argued that $B_1 < B_2$ because $A_1 > A_2$ (e.g., in the case of comparing the times of the Lego trains, some students claimed that the taller/heavier train travels faster while others claimed that the smaller/lighter train travels faster). The mere existence of the second type of response seems to contradict our claim that students judge according to the rule "More A ($A_1 > A_2$)–More B ($B_1 > B_2$)." However, when we examine students' actual responses of this type, we find that they relate to the natural opposites of A, and not to A itself (for instance, instead of relating to the taller train, they relate to the shorter one, arguing that "the shorter–the faster"; similarly, instead of relating to the heavier train, they relate to the lighter one). Clearly, such responses are manifestations of the intuitive rule.

We have shown that comparison tasks in which the two objects or systems are perceptually different with respect to a certain quantity, A, elicit a specific pattern of response ($B_1 > B_2$ because $A_1 > A_2$). We believe this response is directly activated by immediate perceptual differences in quantity A (e.g., length, mass, etc.) or by salient differences between symbols associated with perceptual images in this quantity (e.g., numbers). Our claim is that subjects' cognitive systems are affected by the irrelevant perceptual differences in quantity A, leading them to regard this quantity as the significant one in the problem. It seems that our cognitive system tacitly assumes that the two objects differ in the same direction as quantity A with regard to other quantities as well. This assumption could evolve from a more general tendency to extrapolate. In the case of the intuitive rule "More A–More B," the response $B_1 > B_2$ is extrapolated from $A_1 > A_2$. Even though this extrapolation is valid in many situations, it is not so in others. We regard "More A–More B" as a basic, logical cognitive scheme that is used indiscriminately, resulting in overgeneralizations.

What Is the Origin of the Tendency to Extrapolate from $A_1 > A_2$ to $B_1 > B_2$?

At this stage we can suggest two speculative possibilities.

It Is an Innate Tendency

A considerable number of researchers have suggested the existence of innate concepts and schemes. For instance, Fodor (1975) claims that all lexical concepts are innate. Jackendoff (1989) and Weirzbicka (1980) suggest that all concepts arise from a small set of universal innate primitives. Spelke (1991) argues that the initial representation of physical objects remains at the core of a mature conception of object. Lately, it has been suggested that a rudimentary number sense is wired into our brain at birth (Butterworth, 1999; Dehaene, 1997; Dehaene, Spelke, Pinel, Stanescu, & Tsivkin, 1999). The following anecdotal excerpt, taken from Tinbergen's (1955) book on the study of instinct in animals, suggests the possibility that the intuitive rule "More A–More B" is innate:

> Oystercatchers preferred a clutch of 5 eggs to the normal clutch of three. Still more astonishing is the oystercatchers' preference for abnormally large eggs. If presented with an egg with normal oystercatcher size, one of herring gull's size, and one double the (linear) size of the herring gull's egg, the majority of choices fall upon the largest egg. (p. 45)

It seems that the oystercatchers' decisions are determined by implicit laws of "the more (eggs)–the better (chance of survival)" and "the larger (the egg)–the better (chance of survival)."

It Is an Acquired Tendency, Based on Successful Experiences

As mentioned earlier in this chapter, the rule "More A–More B" is often applicable both in everyday life and in school situations. Children, from early infancy, encounter many situations in which perceptual differences between two objects go hand in hand with parallel quantitative differences in another property of these objects.

At this stage in our inquiries, it is impossible to determine the origin of this intuitive rule. Yet repeated experience seems to reinforce it, thus enhancing its use in other seemingly similar situations.

Why Do We Relate to "More A–More B" as Intuitive?

We regard this type of response as intuitive because problem solvers often view it as self-evident. Furthermore, the use of the rule is often accompanied by a sense of confidence. Self-evidence and confidence are two major characteristics of intuitive reasoning (Fischbein, 1987).

How Do We Overcome the Effects of the Rule?

We have mentioned before that the rule is often used in situations in which it is not applicable. Yet, we have shown that with regard to many of the tasks described in this chapter, children and adults at different ages and/or with different levels of instruction at some point start using the rule selectively.

Young children are very strongly affected by the rule, applying it even when information about the equality in quantity B is perceptually given (see, for instance, the cases of angle and time). Later on, children can disregard irrelevant perceptual information (in quantity A) and correctly judge that although $A_1 > A_2$, B_1 is equal to or smaller than B_2. But even then they are still affected by the intuitive rule in situations in which logical schemes (e.g., conservation, proportion) are needed for correct judgment. And when children acquire these logical schemes, they are still affected by the rule when scientific, formal knowledge is the main source for correct responses (e.g., infinite sets, free-fall, cell size).

More generally, we suggest that with age and/or instruction, schemes, rules, and bodies of knowledge related to specific tasks are developed or reinforced. Consequently, in respect to these tasks, the rule loses its power in favor of other, competing knowledge. For instance, in the case of the conservation of quantity of matter, "the higher–the more" is replaced by considerations of identity or compensation. It is also possible that with age and/or instruction, children become aware of the need to examine their initial responses, to consider other factors that might be relevant to the task, and to avoid conflicting arguments. Thus, they gradually learn the limits within which "More A–More B" is applicable.

Although children cease to use the rule in certain instances at certain ages, they never stop using it altogether, and it continues to dominate in various other situations. In fact, in many of the previously described instances (e.g., comparing segments, comparing angles, free-fall) older children and adults kept using the rule, even after formal, related instruction.

Many of the tasks described here are either classical Piagetian tasks or somewhat similar to such tasks. In Piaget's numerous writings, responses of the type "More A–More B" are often described, and they are ascribed to the intuitive preoperational stage. Piaget explains: "It is obvious that the reason for the non-conservation of physical matter must be the same as that of mathematical entities: The primacy of direct perception over intellectual operations" (Piaget & Inhelder, 1974, p. 9). Our approach coincides with Piaget's in regard to the primacy of direct perception at young ages. Yet we regard a response of the type "More A–More B" as a basic, intuitive logical scheme because it forms a quantitative relationship between two quantities.

We also argue that the use of this logical scheme does not entirely vanish with age.

Support for the possibility that the intuitive rule persists even after formal instruction comes from the following example: A very distinguished physics professor, an expert in astronomy, answering a question on a television science program, was heard to explain that "the force that the larger star exerts on its moon is larger than the force that the moon exerts on the star." Of course this professor was familiar with Newton's third law (the law of action and reaction), according to which any two bodies exert the same force on each other. The next day, he explained that because of his agitation at appearing on television, he had given an immediate, uncontrolled response. Such regressions to intuitive rules are very common.

2

Learning About the Intuitive Rule
"Same A–Same B"

This chapter, like the previous one, deals with situations in which people are asked to compare two quantities and to determine whether they are equal or not. In the previous chapter we showed that students often use the intuitive rule "More A–More B" when the objects (or systems) to be compared *differ* in a certain salient quantity, A. When students are asked to compare the objects (or systems) with respect to another quantity, B, for which B_1 is not greater than B_2, a substantial number of them respond incorrectly, according to the rule "More A (the salient quantity)–More B (the quantity in question)."

In this chapter we explore situations in which the two objects (or systems) to be compared *are equal* in respect to a certain quantity, A ($A_1 = A_2$), but differ in another quantity, B ($B_1 \neq B_2$). Students are asked to compare B_1 and B_2. We show that in a great variety of comparison tasks involving mathematical or scientific concepts, students often incorrectly argue that $B_1 = B_2$ because $A_1 = A_2$. Our main claim is that such responses are specific instances of another, intuitive rule: "Same A–Same B." This rule is a possible source for many of the reported alternative conceptions in science and mathematics.

We first discuss situations in which the equality in quantity A is directly given in the task and then situations in which the equality in quantity A is not given but can be logically deduced.

DIRECTLY GIVEN EQUALITY

John, who works in a large department store, wants to buy his child a computer as a birthday present. He knows that the department store intends to raise the price of this computer by 10% and that 2 weeks later, all toys will be on sale with 10% off. His child's birthday will occur during the sale time. John and his wife, Anna, discuss when it is better to buy the computer:

immediately (before prices go up) or during the sale. John suggests buying the computer immediately, before the price goes up. He claims that because both the price increase and the reduction will be 10%, the price will be the same before the increase and during the sale. Anna, however, says that it will be cheaper to buy the computer during the sale.

John's claim sounds very convincing. Indeed, the increase and the reduction are both 10%. However, Anna is right in this case. To explain it, let's assume, for instance, that the price of the computer is $2000. After the 10% increase, the cost will be $2200. After the sale deduction of 10% ($220), the price will be $1980, so that the family will save $20.

In similar situations involving percentages, many people would react the way John did, assuming that "the same percent–the same amount of money." This is one instance in which the intuitive rule "Same A (same percent)–Same B (same amount of money)" is used.

In this case the equality in quantity A is explicitly given in the problem. It is the very same percentage (10%). Similar reactions ("Same A–Same B") were observed in a variety of situations not necessarily involving percentages.

Let's, for instance, discuss the following cases.

Length and distance. Piaget and colleagues (1960) asked young children to compare the length of a straight line with that of a wavy line. The lines were of different lengths, but they began and finished at parallel points on the page. Piaget and colleagues reported that 84% of children aged 4 to 5 incorrectly replied that the lines were equal in length. A typical response was: "They are both the same length [indicating the endpoints]." The researchers interpreted this response by referring to children's development of the concept of length. They argued that "at this stage, the length of a line is estimated solely in terms of its endpoints without reference to its rectilinearity" (p. 92). We may also regard this response as a case in which the intuitive rule "Same A (distance between endpoints)–Same B (length of lines)" is activated.

In this case, the equality in quantity A (distance between endpoints) was perceptually given and no numbers were mentioned in the task. The situation of John and Anna, mentioned earlier, related to prices, and there the equality in quantity A was expressed in numerical terms. We now consider another situation in which the equality in quantity A is expressed in numerical terms.

Concentration and temperature. Children aged 4 to 14 were presented with two cups of water and were asked about the relative sweetness of the water after sugar was added to both cups. One cup was full of water, and 1 teaspoon of sugar was mixed into it. The same amount of sugar was added to the other same-sized but half-full cup. The children were asked whether they thought the sweetness of the sugarwater in the two cups would be the same or not and, if not, in which cup the water would be sweeter (Figure 2.1).

This task was included in a study on the development of children's conception of concentration (sweetness) conducted by Stavy and colleagues (1982). Most of the young participants (4- to 8-year-olds) argued that because each cup contained water and 1 teaspoon of sugar, they must be equally sweet.

Very similar results were obtained in regard to the development of children's conceptions of temperature (Ravia, 1992; Stavy & Berkovitz, 1980; Strauss & Stavy, 1982). Children were asked (1) to compare the temperature of different amounts of water heated by the same number of candles for the same duration of time and (2) to compare the temperature of different amounts of water cooled by the same number of ice cubes. Young children (4- to 9-year-olds) incorrectly claimed that "the temperature of the water in the two cups is equal because both were heated by the same number of candles" and that "the temperature of the water in the two cups is equal because both are cooled by the same number of ice cubes." Starting from age 9, most children correctly judged the relative temperatures of the heated water and that of the cooled water.

The behaviors of the young children in these studies were often interpreted as resulting from nondifferentiation between mass and concentration or nondifferentiation between heat and temperature (Erickson, 1979; Wiser & Carey, 1983). Another explanation related to children's difficulty in coping with inverse ratio in the context of intensive quantities (Noelting, 1980a, 1980b; Strauss & Stavy, 1982). Our claim is that such incorrect responses could be viewed as applications of the general rule "Same A (same amount of sugar/ice cubes/candles)–Same B (same sweetness/temperature)."

So far, we have shown that the rule "Same A–Same B" can explain students' responses that were previously described as alternative conceptions

Figure 2.1 Concentration: Inverse Ratio

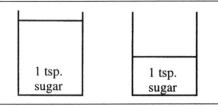

in the mathematics and science education research literature. In order to test the predictive power of this rule, we specially designed several tasks. In these tasks, students were presented with two objects (or systems) that were equal in respect to a certain quantity A ($A_1 = A_2$) but differed in another quantity B ($B_1 \neq B_2$). Students were asked to compare B_1 and B_2. The equality in quantity A was explicitly mentioned in the task.

Rectangles. Mendel (1998) presented eleventh-grade students with a problem involving percentages and perimeters (Figure 2.2). Only 8% of the students knew that the perimeter of the rectangle after the change is smaller because "a is bigger than b, and decreasing 20% of it is more than adding 20% of b." The vast majority of the students (72%) claimed that the perimeter remains the same because "you added 20% and removed the same percentage, so they compensate each other."

As mentioned earlier, many people react the same way in similar situations involving percentages. Such a response is often interpreted with reference to students' misconceptions of percentages, as evidence of their failure to understand that percentages cannot be compared without taking into account what they refer to (van den Heuvel-Panhuizen, 1994). Clearly, this response, too, is of the kind "Same A (same percent)–Same B (same perimeter)."

Rate of cooling. Livne (1996) presented students with the task shown in Figure 2.3. Clearly, the cylindrical bottle will cool faster because the rate of cooling depends on the ratio of surface area to volume. In this task the amount of milk in the two bottles is the same ($A_1 = A_2 = 100$ ml), and therefore we predict that a substantial number of students will judge that "same amount of milk–same rate of cooling."

Figure 2.2 Percentages and Perimeters

Consider the following rectangle:

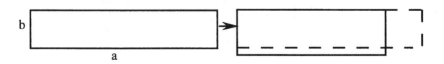

Side a is reduced by 20% and side b is increased by 20%.
Is the perimeter of the rectangle before the change bigger than/equal to/smaller than the perimeter of the rectangle after the change?

Figure 2.3 Surface Area and Rate of Cooling

Debby is a baby-sitter. The baby she is watching wakes up crying, and Debby wants to feed her. She realizes that the milk she has heated is too hot and wants to cool it as fast as possible. She has two differently shaped bottles, a ball-shaped one and a cylinder-shaped one. Each bottle can contain 100 ml. She fills each bottle with 100 ml of milk (up to the nipple) and immerses them both in ice water.

What is your opinion? Is the time needed to cool the milk in the spherical bottle equal to/not equal to the time needed to cool the milk in the cylindrical bottle? If you think that the time is not equal, in which bottle does the milk cool faster? Why?

This problem was presented to Israeli biology majors in grades 10, 11, and 12. Fewer than 50% of the students at each grade level based their judgment on the ratio between surface area and volume and therefore knew that the cylindrical bottle would cool faster. As predicted, a non-negligible number of students (29%, 31%, and 38% of the students in grades 10, 11, and 12, respectively) argued that "*The time needed to cool the milk in both bottles is equal* because *the amounts of milk in each bottle are equal.*" Although these students have learned about the ratio of surface area to volume and its role in biological systems, their response was of the type "Same A (amount of milk)–Same B (rate of cooling)." These responses of mature students with a relatively high level of biology education suggest that the rule "Same A–Same B" has coercive power.

Resistance of bacteria. In the previous problem, the equality in quantity A was expressed by a number (100 ml). Livne (1996) presented the same students with another task related to surface area and volume, one in which the equality in quantity A was mentioned but no numbers were given, as shown in Figure 2.4.

Students' responses to this task resembled their responses to the task related to the cooling of milk. About 40% of the students recognized the surface area/volume ratio and correctly claimed that the spherical bacteria are the most resistant to dryness. However, about a third of the students

Figure 2.4 Surface Area and Resistance of Bacteria

The common shapes of bacteria are spherical (cocci), rod-like (bacilli), and spiral (spirillae). The following drawing depicts bacteria from each of these three types:

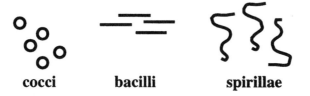

cocci   **bacilli**   **spirillae**

The cell volume of these bacteria *is equal*. Is the resistance to dryness of these three types of differently shapes bacteria equal/nonequal? Explain your answer.
If you think their resistance is different, which of these three types of bacteria is most resistant? Why?

---

claimed, in accordance with the intuitive rule, that "the cells have the *same volume* and therefore their *resistance to dryness is the same*," thus arriving at an incorrect solution.

Angles in polygons. Another task in which the equality in quantity A was explicitly mentioned but no numbers were given is shown in Figure 2.5. Rojhany (1997) presented this task to children in grades 4, 6, 8, and 10. The correct answer is that angle 1 is bigger than angle 2, but we predicted that because of the equality of the sides of the two polygons and/or the overall similarity between the two drawn objects, many students would claim that "same sides–same angles."

About 50% of the students in grades 4, 6, and 8, and a substantial number in grade 10 (25%), incorrectly claimed that the two angles were equal. The most typical justification of the younger students (grades 4, 6, and 8) was: "The sides are equal, so the angles are equal." This response directly reflects application of the intuitive rule "Same A–Same B" to this specific situation. The older students, who had studied Euclidean geometry, used more elaborate justifications, for example, "in a triangle, the angles opposite equal sides are equal" or "if each of the two polygons were to be bounded by a circle, the chords of the two resulting circles would be equal, and, in accordance with the theorem related to angles and equal chords, the angles would be equal as well." These students used geometrical, theorem-like statements, all in line with the intuitive rule "Same A–Same B." Possibly, the construction of these theorem-like statements results from students' attempts to account for their intuitive judgment according to the intuitive

Figure 2.5 Polygons and Angles

Consider a regular pentagon and a regular hexagon. The length of the sides of the pentagon are equal to the length of the sides of the hexagon.

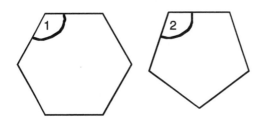

Circle your answer:
a. Angle 1 is bigger than angle 2.
b. Angle 2 is bigger than angle 1.
c. Angle 1 is equal to angle 2.
d. It is impossible to determine.
Explain your choice.

---

rule "Same A–Same B." The evident result is overgeneralization of geometrical theorems.

In this task, the two regular polygons were equal in respect to one quantity (the length of the sides), but they differed in another quantity (the number of sides). Students were asked to compare the two polygons with reference to a third quantity—the size of the angles. Here, students could either react in accordance with the second intuitive rule "Same A (length of sides)–Same B (size of angles)" or in accordance with the first intuitive rule "More A (number of sides)–More B (size of angles)." A substantial number of students responded incorrectly, in accordance with the second intuitive rule. Thus it seems that although the use of the first intuitive rule coincides with the correct answer, the participating students were more affected by the equality in the length of the sides than by the inequality in the number of sides. Possibly, the similarity in the overall appearance of the two objects contributed to the dominance of the second intuitive rule.

Cubes. In the following example, no quantitative equality was involved, but the two objects shared a qualitative property (i.e., shape). In the task presented in Figure 2.6, the surface area/volume ratio of cube 1 is larger than the surface area/volume ratio of cube 2.

Figure 2.6 Surface Area/Volume of Different-Sized Cubes

Consider two different-sized cubes. Is the ratio between the surface area and volume of cube 1 larger than/equal to/smaller than the ratio between the surface area and volume of cube 2? Explain your answer.

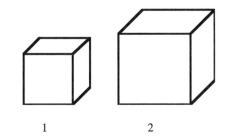

1   2

Again, our prediction was that students would be affected by the identity in shape and would claim that "same shape (cube)–same ratio (surface area/volume)." This task was also included in Livne's (1996) study, whose participants were biology majors in grades 10, 11, and 12. As predicted, substantial percentages (41%, 45%, and 55%, respectively) incorrectly argued that the surface area/volume ratio in the cubes is the same. Typical explanations were: "Cube 1 and cube 2 have the same geometrical shape; hence the ratio of surface area to volume in both cubes is the same regardless of their size" or "The surface area and the volume in cube 1 are proportionally smaller than in cube 2 and therefore the ratio is constant." In the first justification, students explicitly referred to the shared qualitative property—shape. In the second justification, "formal" schemes such as proportion were invoked in an attempt to support the judgment.

This task involves a situation in which the two objects have the same shape but differ in size. One could expect that a substantial number of students would be affected by the difference in size and incorrectly claim, in accordance with the first intuitive rule, that "the surface area/volume ratio in the larger cube is larger." Livne's data show that when asked to compare the surface area/volume ratio, students were more affected by the similarity in the shape (cube) than by the difference in volume. In fact, only 24%, 19%, and 24% of the students in grades 10, 11, and 12, respectively, claimed that the surface area/volume ratio is larger in cube 2 than in cube 1. Possibly, when students of these ages are asked to compare the ratio between two quantities (surface area/volume), each of which increases with the size of the object, they assume that this ratio remains the same. These last examples demonstrate the strong predictive power of the intuitive rule "Same A–Same B."

By now, we hope we have supplied enough convincing evidence regarding the power of this intuitive rule. We have shown that it determines children's and adults' judgments in comparison tasks related to various topics, concepts, and content domains in science and mathematics.

The following section provides further evidence for the strong effect of this rule on students' ways of thinking in other types of situations. In these situations the equality in quantity A is not given, but it can be logically derived by either the conservation scheme or the proportion scheme.

LOGICALLY DEDUCED EQUALITY

We have shown that the intuitive rule "Same A–Same B" is activated in comparison tasks in which two systems (or objects) are equal in a certain quantity, A ($A_1 = A_2$), and differ in another quantity, B ($B_1 \neq B_2$).

In all the tasks described so far, the equality in quantity A was explicitly given (perceptually, in numerical or verbal terms, or in qualitative properties). If our claim is correct that the rule "Same A–Same B" is triggered in comparison tasks by the equality in quantity A, then we may expect that the rule will also be activated when this equality is not directly given but is logically deduced. In this section we examine this hypothesis.

Two logical schemes that can lead to equality judgments in certain tasks are conservation and proportion. Piaget suggested that these two schemes develop with age: The conservation scheme develops during the concrete operational stage and the proportion scheme during the formal operational stage (Inhelder & Piaget, 1958; Piaget & Inhelder, 1974). In this section we examine several tasks in which the equality in quantity A can be deduced through the conservation or the proportion scheme ($A_1 = A_2$). We show that realization of equality, based on these two logical schemes, activates the rule "Same A–Same B"; that is, once students conserve a certain quantity, they will also "conserve" other quantities that are actually not conserved under the specific circumstances. Similarly, students who deduce, on the basis of the proportion scheme, that two given ratios are equal will also claim that other related quantities are equal.

Conservation

Surface area and volume of two cylinders. Let us think about the questions relating to the surface area and volume of the two cylinders presented in Figure 2.7. The first question is a classical Piagetian task involving conservation of area. Clearly, the areas of the two sheets are equal ($S_1 = S_2$).

Figure 2.7 Cylinders: Surface Area and Volume

Take two identical rectangular (nonsquare) sheets of papers (sheet 1 and sheet 2):
✔ Rotate one sheet (sheet 2 by 90°)
  Is the area of sheet 1 equal to/larger than/smaller than the area of sheet 2? Explain your answer.
✔ Fold each sheet (as show in the drawing).
  You get two cylinders: cylinder 1 and cylinder 2.
  Is the volume of cylinder 1 equal to/larger than/smaller than the volume of cylinder 2? Explain your answer

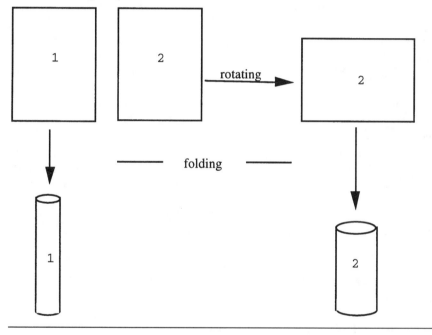

How can one compare the volumes of these two cylinders?

It is possible to empirically compare the volumes by, for example, pouring sand into both cylinders and comparing the amounts of sand needed for filling each of them. If you try this, you will find that the amount of sand needed to fill cylinder 2 is larger than that needed to fill cylinder 1. The same conclusion could also be reached by applying the formula for calculating the volume of cylinders ($\pi r^2 h$) and observing that r is raised to the second power while h is not.

Our hypothesis about students' responses to this task is that when students start to conserve the area of the two sheets of paper, they will also argue, in line with the intuitive rule "Same A–Same B," that the volumes of the two cylinders are equal. To test this hypothesis, we presented K–9 students with the task described above (Ronen, in press).

Our findings in respect to the task involving conservation of area are similar to those reported by Piaget and colleagues (1960). High percentages of kindergartners and first-graders (95% and 67%, respectively) incorrectly argued that the areas of the rectangles, after rotating sheet 2, are not equal. Most of them argued, in line with the first intuitive rule, that "the longer (the side)–the larger (the area)" or "the taller (the side)–the larger (the area)." From second grade on, the vast majority of the children conserved the area. Most of them based their judgments on identity, reversibility, additivity, and compensation arguments (e.g., "It's the same paper"; "You can turn it back and see that it's the same"). This change in behavior is explained by Piaget and colleagues (1960) as resulting from the development of the logical conservation-of-area scheme.

Our data show a gradual increase from kindergarten to grade 5 in the percentages of students who incorrectly argued that *the volumes of the two cylinders are equal* ("conservation" of volume). Most kindergartners and first-graders (95% and 80%, respectively) argued that the volumes of cylinder 1 and cylinder 2 differ. The vast majority of them incorrectly claimed that "the volume of the taller cylinder is larger." From grade 2 to grade 5, there is a gradual decrease in the percentages of students who incorrectly claimed that "the taller–the larger" and a parallel increase in the percentages of those who argued that the volumes of the two cylinders are the same. A very small percentage of the students in the upper grades correctly argued that the volume of cylinder 2 is larger than that of cylinder 1, while the others at these grade levels (at least 83%) incorrectly claimed that the volumes of the two cylinders are equal.

Most equality judgments were justified by the claim that "the volumes of the two cylinders are *the same* because they are made *from the same sheets of papers*" or, similarly, that "the volumes of the two cylinders are *the same* because *the areas of the sheets are the same.*" Another argument, based on compensation reasoning and more frequently mentioned by the older students, was that "the volumes are the same because one cylinder is taller but thinner than the other." These explanations are those typically given to conservation tasks.

At the beginning of this section, we hypothesized that children's realization of equality in quantity A ($A_1 = A_2$) in conservation tasks may activate the use of the rule "Same A–Same B." Our results confirm this hypothesis. Indeed, students who conserved the area "conserved" the volume as well. The similarity between the graphs describing the development of the conservation of area and the "conservation" of volume is striking. Moreover, starting from grade 5, most children "conserved" both area and volume, and there is no evidence of a decrease with age in students' incorrect judgments about "conservation" of volume.

Evidence for the role of the intuitive rule "Same A–Same B" can be found in other cases related to mathematics and science. Here we provide some examples.

Area and perimeter of geometric shapes. Consider the "thread" task presented in Figure 2.8. Children in grades K to 9 were presented with this task. Here again, a notable number of children who conserved the length "conserved" the area as well. Students who conserved both the perimeter and the area mainly used identity arguments to justify their answers to the area task (e.g., "It's the same thread, therefore it's the same area"). As in the previous task, the percentages of incorrect, equality responses increased with age (Ronen, in press).

The same students were presented with a "cut-and-paste" task related to the same quantities: perimeter and area (Figure 2.9). In this problem, the area was conserved but the perimeter was not. It is reasonable to assume that the obvious perceptual differences between the perimeters of the two rectangles would support correct responses (i.e., "the perimeter of the cut-and-paste rectangle is larger"). Indeed, the vast majority of the young children (kindergartners and first-graders) correctly judged that the perimeter of

Figure 2.8 Geometric Shapes: Perimeter and Area

✔ Compare the length and the area bounded by two identical closed threads put into the same rectangular shape.

✔ Change the shape of one of the threads to make a circle.

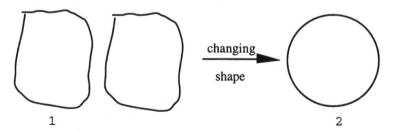

Are the lengths of the two threads (1 and 2) the same or different? If different, which is longer? Why? Are the areas bounded by the threads (1 and 2) the same or different? If different, which is larger?

Why?

Figure 2.9 Rectangles: Area and Perimeter

Compare the perimeters and areas of two identical sheets of paper before and after cutting one of them and pasting the two cut parts together again in a different shape.

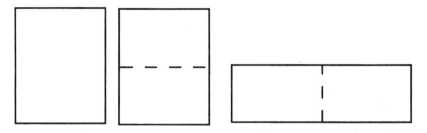

the cut-and-paste rectangle is larger than that of the original one. However, older children who conserved the area disregarded these perceptually obvious differences, incorrectly arguing, in line with the intuitive rule "Same A–Same B," that the perimeters of the two rectangles are equal. This response increased with grade level and was frequent in the upper grades. Typical justifications were: "It's the same paper; therefore the perimeter is the same" or "It's the same area; therefore the perimeter is the same." This behavior indicates the coercive power of the intuitive rule "Same A–Same B" as it successfully competes with direct, perceptual contradictory information.

Both the thread and cut-and-paste tasks involve the same geometrical concepts (area and perimeter). In each of them, the identity of the involved objects is evident (the same thread, the same sheet of paper). We have shown that students' responses to these tasks were strongly affected by the intuitive rule "Same A–Same B." The differences between the two graphs (conservation of area, "conservation" of perimeter) in the cut-and-paste task is larger than the differences between the graphs (conservation of perimeter, "conservation" of area) in the thread problem. Possibly, the visual information in the cut-and-paste problem supported the correct judgment (i.e., that the perimeter of the cut-and-paste rectangle is larger). Such supporting visual information was not available in the thread problem. The observed differences in the students' responses in these tasks suggest that visual information contradicting the rule may somewhat suppress the rule's effects.

The mathematics education literature reports that many students and adults adhere to the view that shapes with the same perimeters must have the same area, and vice versa. Incorrect responses of the type "same area–same perimeter" or "same perimeter–same area" were reported in many studies on students' misconceptions in geometry (e.g., Dembo, Levin, & Siegler, 1997; Hirstein, 1981; Hoffer & Hoffer, 1992; Linchevsky, 1985; Shultz,

Dover, & Amsel, 1979; Walter, 1970; Woodward & Byrd, 1983). These studies interpreted students' responses as resulting from a misunderstanding of the relationship between the concepts of area and perimeter. Our claim is that this response could be viewed, in a broader perspective, as being determined by the application of the general intuitive rule "Same A–Same B," which is related not only to area and perimeter but also to many other quantities.

These tasks dealt with mathematical objects. The study conducted by Ronen (in press) included other tasks, related to material objects.

Weight and volume of water. Ronen (in press) presented children in grades K to 9 with two vials containing equal amounts of water. Both vials were corked, and a tube was inserted through the cork. One of the vials was heated, the water expanded, and, consequently, its level rose in the tube. The difference between the levels of water in the two tubes was visible (Figure 2.10). The children were asked to compare the weights and the volumes of water in the two vials before and after heating. In this case, the weight of the water was conserved ($W_1 = W_2$) but the volume, after heating, was larger ($V_2 > V_1$).

We found that children below grade 4 did not conserve the weight, claiming that the heated water weighed more than the unheated water because "the level of water is higher." (Similar results were reported by Megged [1978]; and by Piaget and Inhelder [1974].) From grade 5 on, most students correctly judged that the weight of the water in the two vials was

Figure 2.10 Expansion: Weight and Volume

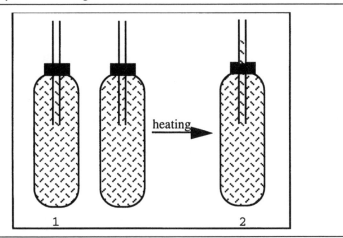

the same, arguing that "it's the same water, and it was only heated" or "nothing was added or subtracted."

In respect to the volumes before and after heating, most children in the lower grades correctly judged that the volume of the heated water was larger, claiming that "the level of water is higher." Most sixth- and seventh-graders claimed that the volume of the heated water was equal to that of the unheated water, explaining that "it's the same water, therefore it's the same volume." In the upper grades there was an increase in correct judgments, accompanied by reference to the particulate nature of matter.

These data show that at certain grades students "conserved" both weight and volume. These high percentages of reasoning that "the same water–the same weight–the same volume" suggest once more the coercive effect of the intuitive rule "Same A–Same B," which in this case, until a certain age, overrules obvious perceptual input. Some students even explicitly said that perceptual differences may mislead and should not be relied on. For instance, Gil, a ninth-grader, explained: "If I was not here when you heated the water, I would have wrongly said that the volume of the heated water is larger. However, I was here and I know that it's the same water; you only heated it and therefore the volumes must be the same." The decrease in responses based on "conservation" of volume and the parallel increase in correct responses might result from instruction related to the particulate nature of matter. Visual information in combination with instruction probably constrain the use of the rule "Same A–Same B" (the particulate theory of matter was studied in grade 7).

All the examples described so far in this section are those of students in grade 9 or below. We now demonstrate that the rule also affects older students' responses to comparison tasks.

Volume and surface area of two rectangular boxes. Livne (1996) asked Israeli biology majors in grades 10, 11, and 12 to compare the volume and the surface area of a box before and after dividing it into four boxes (Figure 2.11). In this case, the volume is conserved but the (total) surface area of the four boxes is larger than that of the initial box. All the participating students conserved the volume, and about 30% "conserved" the surface area as well, claiming that "the boxes derive from the same box" or "if we add all the surfaces we will get the whole" or "nothing was added or subtracted." These data confirm that even high school students are affected by the intuitive rule "Same A (volume)–Same B (surface area)."

We have so far related to one logical scheme, namely, conservation. We have shown that students who started conserving a certain quantity often "conserved" another quantity that in fact was not conserved in the specific

Figure 2.11 Boxes: Volume and Surface Area

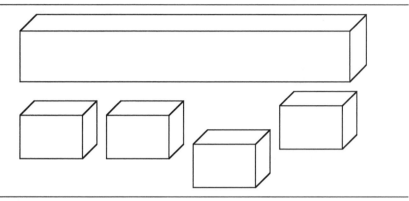

manipulation; their argument was that "Same A (the quantity conserved)– Same B (a quantity not conserved)."

> Are there any other instances in which an acquired logical scheme, which leads to an equality judgment, activates the intuitive rule "Same A–Same B," leading to incorrect overgeneralized judgments?

> Is the use of the rule "Same A–Same B" associated only with the conservation scheme or is it also activated when equality in quantity A ($A_1 = A_2$) is deduced through another logical scheme?

We now examine the scheme of proportion.

Proportion

In the context of the development of probabilistic thinking, Schrage (1983) and Fischbein and Schnarch (1997) asked students to respond to the problem presented in Table 2.1. The table also presents the results reported by Fischbein and Schnarch.

This task is a variation of a classical probability task related to births in two hospitals (Tversky & Kahneman, 1972). According to the law of large numbers, as the sample size (or the number of trials) increases, the relative frequencies tend toward the theoretical probabilities $\left(\frac{1}{2}\right)$. Consequently, the probability of getting heads at least twice in tossing three coins

Table 2.1 Distribution, by Grade, of Students' Responses to Comparison of Probabilities (in %)

	Grades			
The problem	5	7	9	11
The likelihood of getting heads at least twice when tossing three coins is				
smaller than	5	5	25	10
equal to	30	45	60	75
greater than	35	30	10	5
The likelihood of getting heads at least 200 times out of 300 times:				
other answers	5	10	0	0
no answers	25	10	5	10

is greater than that of getting at least 200 heads out of 300 tosses. However, as can be seen from Table 2.1, a substantial number of students at each grade level argued that the probabilities are equal (the frequency of this incorrect response increased with age). These students claimed that $\frac{2}{3} = \frac{200}{300}$ and therefore the probabilities are the same.

In terms of intuitive rules, we explain this behavior as follows: The equivalence in ratios, which is logically deduced through the proportion scheme, activates the intuitive rule "Same A (proportion)–Same B (probability)." Fischbein and Schnarch (1997) similarly explained:

> The principle of equivalence of ratio imposes itself as relevant to the problem and thus dictates the answer. It is the evolution of this principle that shapes the evolution of the related misconception and causes it to become stronger as the student ages. (p. 103)

The increase in the frequency of such responses follows the acquisition and stabilization of the proportion scheme.

We presented a somewhat similar problem to students in grades 7 to 12:

> The Carmel family has two children, and the Levin family has four children. Is the probability that Carmels have one son and one daughter larger than/equal to/smaller than the probability that the Levins have two sons and two daughters? Explain your choice.

In this case, the correct answer could be reached by relatively simple counting and calculation. One has to calculate the ratio between the number of successful events in each family (one son/one daughter in the Carmel family, two sons/two daughters in the Levin family) and the number of all possible combinations of sons and daughters in each of these families. The corresponding ratios are 1 : 2 for the Carmel family and 3 : 8 for the Levin family. Thus, the probability that the Carmel family has one son and one daughter is larger than the probability that there are two daughters and two sons in the Levin family.

We predicted that students would claim that since the target ratio of boys to girls in the two families is the same (1 : 2), the probability would therefore be the same, too (i.e., "same ratio–same probability"). The percentages of correct answers were relatively low at all grade levels, not exceeding 46%. Interestingly, although this problem could be solved by relatively simple means and does not demand advanced knowledge of probability (i.e., the law of large numbers), the graph of equality responses to this problem resembles that in the previous problem.

These examples confirm that the activation of the intuitive rule "Same A–Same B" is not limited to conservation tasks. The question of whether there are other cases in which a logically deduced equality activates the use of the rule "Same A–Same B" still remains open, however.

SOME QUESTIONS ABOUT THE USE OF THIS RULE

In this chapter, we presented students' responses to a variety of comparison tasks in mathematics and science. Many of them had been previously described in the research literature, either in the context of the development of specific mathematical and scientific concepts or in that of the development of logical schemes. As regards the first context (e.g., percentages, concentration, area, perimeter, volume, temperature), students' responses were explained with reference to the central notions under discussion (e.g., being aware or unaware of the relative nature of percentages). In the literature on the development of logical schemes, tasks related to conservation and proportion were presented to children by Piaget and many others in an attempt to study the development of these schemes and their acquisition. These tasks related to various quantities, including area, volume, mass, number, and so forth. Students' responses were interpreted as reflecting their developmental stage.

All tasks discussed in this chapter were similar: In each of them, the two objects or systems to be compared were equal in respect to one quality or quantity ($A_1 = A_2$) but differed in respect to another quantity ($B_1 \neq B_2$).

Children were asked to compare the two objects or systems with regard to quantity B. In some of the tasks, the equality in quantity A was perceptually or directly given. In other cases, the equality in quantity A could be logically derived through the scheme of conservation or proportion. A common incorrect response to all these tasks, regardless of the content domain, took the form of $B_1 = B_2$ because $A_1 = A_2$.

We regard all these responses as specific instances of the use of the intuitive rule "Same A–Same B." We have shown that common external characteristics of the tasks dictate a specific pattern of response ($B_1 = B_2$ because $A_1 = A_2$). It seems that our cognitive system tacitly assumes that when two objects are equal in a certain quantity, they are equal in other quantities as well. This assumption could evolve from a more general tendency to extrapolate given information to new situations. In the case of the intuitive rule "Same A–Same B," the response $B_1 = B_2$ is extrapolated from explicitly given or logically derived information about the equality in quantity A. This type of extrapolation, although valid in many situations, does not apply to others.

Why Do We Call It an Intuitive Rule?

This rule has the characteristics of an intuitive rule (Fischbein, 1987) because the response "Same A–Same B" seems self-evident (subjects perceive statements they made on the basis of this rule as being true and in need of no further justification). Moreover, the rule is used with great confidence and perseverance (often persisting in spite of formal learning that contradicts it). And finally, the rule has attributes of globality (subjects tend to apply it to diverse situations) and coerciveness (alternatives are often excluded as unacceptable).

What Factors Affect the Application of This Rule?

The rule "Same A–Same B" appears to be applied in a nonuniform way. In some tasks, only young children respond in accordance with it (e.g., length, concentration, temperature). In other tasks, only older students and adults react according to the rule (e.g., surface area and volume). Clearly, the application of "Same A–Same B" in the logically deduced tasks occurs only after the subjects have acquired the relevant scheme (conservation or proportion). Another observation is that in some cases the incorrect application of the rule increases with age to reach a certain plateau, whereas in other cases there are clear age-related indications of a decrease in application (e.g., weight and volume of water).

Possibly, the application of the rule "Same A–Same B" to a specific comparison task is determined by the interaction of various factors, including (1) the nature of the information about the equality in quantity A (e.g., explicitly given vs. logically deduced) and (2) solver-related characteristics such as age, instruction, repertoire of intuitive rules, logical schemes, and formal knowledge.

Thus, variation in students' responses to the task involving the weight and volume of water, for instance, could be interpreted as follows: The obvious perceptual differences between the volumes of the heated and nonheated water support the use of the intuitive rule "More A–More B," which in this case leads to a correct response regarding the volumes of the water but to an incorrect response regarding the weights. Indeed, the vast majority of the young children correctly judged that the volume of the hot water is larger than that of the cold water but misjudged the weight, claiming that "hot water weighs more than cold water." However, older children, who have already acquired the conservation-of-mass scheme, knew that "the weight of the cold water and the hot water is the same." These students were convinced of this equality, and their judgment was based on logical reasoning. It seems that this realization of identity, which demands overcoming perceptual differences, is very strong. This logically based belief in equality activates the rule "Same A–Same B," leading students to claim that the volume of the heated and nonheated water is the same, despite the obvious perceptual differences in volumes. This incorrect response increases with the stabilization of the conservation scheme and is frequent in the upper grades. Formal instruction in physical science usually directly discusses the phenomenon of expansion of matter. This instruction, together with the obvious perceptual differences, successfully competes with the intuitive rule "Same A–Same B." The ultimate result is an increase in the percentages of correct responses concerning both the volume and the weight. Yet in other problems, such as that concerning the surface area and volume of two cylinders, such a decreased effect of the intuitive rule "Same A–Same B" in the upper grades is not observed. In this latter task, there are no obvious perceptual differences supporting the correct answer, and, usually, instruction related to volume and surface area does not directly relate to aspects that are relevant to this problem.

The development of an incorrect response with age, and its stabilization from about the fifth grade, contradicts the common assumption that cognitive competence advances with age. In the few cases related to conservation in which a decrease in competence with age was observed, it was reported that this decrement was temporary and was followed by a significant increase in competence (e.g., Mehler & Bever, 1967; Strauss, 1982; Strauss & Stavy, 1982). Such decrements, unlike the one observed in this chapter, are viewed by researchers as an essential, intermediate stage in the process of cognitive development. Our interpretation of the phenomenon reported here—in respect to the "conservation" of volume in the cylinder task, the "conservation" of area in the thread task, and the "conservation" of perimeter in the cut-and-paste task—is that the decrement in correct responses and the stabilization of incorrect responses are results of the joint action of students' strong, logically based belief in the equality in quantity A and the coercive power of the intuitive rule "Same A–Same B" on their cognitive system.

What Are the Relations Between the Intuitive Rule "Same A–Same B" and the Scheme of Conservation?

The classical conservation tasks presented here were previously used by Piaget and many others to explore the development of children's understanding of basic concepts in mathematics and science (number, mass, etc.). For Piaget, the conservation of a certain quantity was an indication of the acquisition of the related concept. Piaget assumed that a child who conserved a certain quantity could differentiate between the conserved quantity and other quantities that are not conserved in a certain manipulation (Piaget, 1968). A child who conserved a certain quantity and also "conserved" other quantities that are in fact not conserved in the specific manipulation was regarded as a "pseudo-conserver" of the quantity. Piaget regarded pseudo-conservation as a marginal behavioral phenomenon, occurring before proper conservation.

We found, however, that children, adolescents, and adults alike often manifest this pseudo-conservation. Thus, in Piaget's terms, the vast majority of the population should be regarded as pseudo-conservers in respect to quantities such as area, weight, and volume.

The fact that students at different ages argued, in various conservation tasks, for equality not only in the quantity being conserved, but also in other "nonconserved" quantities, raises some concerns about the meanings and applications of the notion of conservation. We explain such overconservation in the following manner: Once a child understands the identity of an object in a certain manipulation, the intuitive rule "Same A–Same B" comes into action and leads to the conclusion that several quantities, including those that are conserved and those that are not conserved, remain the same.

Our data also raise some reservations regarding the use of classical conservation tasks as the only means to assess students' knowledge of mathematical and scientific concepts. Traditionally, in order to explore students' understanding of a certain concept, they are presented with a task in which the related quantity is conserved in face of an irrelevant manipulation. However, they are usually not presented with a situation in which the specific quantity related to the concept is not conserved. Our results show that it is impossible to deduce whether students understand the concept from their correct response to the classical conservation task. Therefore it is imperative to examine, in respect to a given concept, not only whether students *do conserve* the related quantity when it *is* conserved but also whether they *do not conserve* it when it is *not* conserved.

3

The Nature of the Intuitive Rule "Everything Can Be Divided"

As mentioned previously, comparison tasks are widely used to study the development of students' conceptions in science and mathematics. Of course, other kinds of tasks are used as well.

One common type of task relates to processes of successive division. Such a task has been used to investigate students' conceptions in both mathematics and science. In mathematics it has been used to study students' conceptions of one of the main concepts in the field—infinity (Fischbein, Tirosh, & Hess, 1979; Nunez, 1991; Tall, 1981). A typical task was:

> Consider a line segment. Divide it into two equal parts. Divide one-half into two equal parts. Continue dividing in the same way. Will this process come to an end?

This task was used to find out whether students conceive of a line segment as consisting of an infinite number of points.

In the physical sciences, similar questions related to the successive division of material objects have been used to investigate students' conceptions of matter as particulate (Carey, 1992; Egozi, 1993; Pfundt, 1981; Stern & Mevarech, 1991). A typical question was:

> Consider a copper wire. Divide it into two equal parts. Divide one-half into two equal parts. Continue dividing in the same way. Will this process come to an end?

Before you continue reading, you may want to predict the responses of students, at the concrete operational and the formal operational levels, to these two tasks.

It would be reasonable to assume that children at the concrete operational level will argue, in response to both tasks, that the processes described will come to an end. They will give various practical, concrete reasons for this (e.g., the segments will become too small to be divided). Later on, at the formal operational level, students are more likely to provide correct—different—answers to each problem.

Research confirms this assumption regarding children at the concrete operational level. Surprisingly, it was found that older students, in grades 10 to 12, gave responses that assumed infinity to both tasks. Typical responses were: "These processes can always be repeated; everything can be divided by 2" (Tirosh & Stavy, 1992, 1996).

What could be the source of these unexpected responses?

We suggest that this common response of assuming infinity to be involved in both tasks may evolve from an intuitive rule related to the process of successive division: "Everything can be divided." It seems that this intuitive rule affects students' responses to tasks involving successive division regardless of the specific nature of the object, be it mathematical or material.

In this chapter we show that the intuitive rule "Everything can be divided" is very often used in carrying out tasks involving successive division. We also investigate the extent to which the rule dominates students' thinking in different situations and try to determine various factors that affect its application. This includes factors related to the problem (e.g., content domain, dimension, state of matter, discrete appearance of objects, and the specific nature of the process of successive division) and factors related to the solver (e.g., age/grade level).

In a series of studies, students of different ages were presented with tasks related to the successive division of mathematical, physical, and biological objects (Cohen, 1997; Egozi, 1993; Farkas, 1993; Fischbein, Tirosh, Stavy, & Oster, 1990; Stavy & Tirosh, 1992, 1993a, 1993b; Tirosh & Stavy, 1992, 1996). In these tasks, students were asked whether the described successive division of a specific object would come to an end. The purpose of these studies was to explore how general is the use of the rule "Everything can be divided."

In this chapter, we refer to two types of successive division tasks: repeated halving and decreasing series.

REPEATED HALVING

A line segment. Let's refer to the task mentioned at the beginning of this chapter:

Consider a line segment. Divide it into two equal parts. Divide one-half into two equal parts. Continue dividing in the same way. Will this process come to an end?

This task was introduced to students in grades 7 to 11. Two types of responses were given at all these grade levels—(1) the process is endless, and (2) the process will come to an end. As mentioned earlier, the frequency of the correct response—assuming infinity—increased with grade level and was relatively high in the upper grades.

Three main justifications were given for the response assuming infinity. The dominant one at all grade levels was in line with the rule "Everything can be divided." Typical explanations at all grade levels were that "it's always possible to continue dividing," that "it is always possible to divide by 2," that "you can always divide into smaller parts," and that "there will always be half of something." The second type of justification, given only by the older students, was that "there are an infinite number of points in a line segment." The third, less frequent, justification was that "we'll reach a point, but a point can also be divided."

The response that the process of halving the line segment would come to an end was common among the younger students. These students argued that "we won't be able to divide anymore because the segment will become extremely small." As expected, most of these students referred to the actual process of division and emphasized its practical limitations. A less frequent justification was that "the segment is finite." This justification was probably the result of students' observation that the segment is bounded. Few students in this category added that the segment contained a finite number of points. The third type of justification was that "we won't be able to divide anymore because we'll reach the basic unit of the segment." Some of the students who offered this justification referred to "the atoms of the segment," whereas others referred to points.

It is notable that the percentages of justifications for the correct responses—assuming infinity—that were based on correct mathematical considerations were very low for all grade levels. This suggests that the correct judgment in this case is usually not a result of mathematical considerations. The fact that most correct judgments were justified by "Everything can be divided" hints that the correct judgment is an instance of the application of the intuitive rule.

Copper wire. This task is similar to the previous one, but here the repeatedly halved object is material. In this case the process of repeated halving comes to a halt when it reaches the atomic level (beyond this, the material ceases to exist as such).

Here, much like in the case of the line segment, the frequency of responses assuming infinity increased with grade level. The justifications students gave for their answers to the copper-wire problem were also similar to those given in the case of the line-segment task. Among the justifications given for the answers assuming infinity, the most common, at all grade levels, was that "it is always possible to divide by 2." Frequent explanations were: "Part of the wire will always remain, and it is possible to divide it by 2"; "As long as there is a way to divide the wire into equal parts, small though they may be, there is no reason that there will not be any smaller part"; "Any part can always be divided"; and "There will always be a small, even invisible, particle of copper that can be divided." Another justification, given by only a few students, was that "the wire is infinite." A third justification was that "we'll reach an atom but it, too, can be halved." This last justification could evolve from integrating the idea that "it is always possible to divide by 2" with the particulate theory of matter. Some of these students inappropriately used their knowledge that an atom consists of elementary particles and referred to it as an entity that can be halved. For instance, one student argued: "Everything can be divided by two, but I learned in science that matter consists of a finite number of atoms. When we reach an atom, it will explode and thus the process of division by two will continue forever."

There were three main justifications for the correct answer assuming finity, the most common being that "we won't be able to divide anymore because the wire will become extremely small." Other justifications were that "there are a finite number of atoms in the copper wire" and that "we won't be able to divide anymore because we'll reach a basic unit (an atom) of the copper wire."

As mentioned before, we explain these surprisingly high percentages of older students who thought the material object was infinite as evolving from the intuitive rule "Everything can be divided." A somewhat similar experiment, aimed at exploring children's conceptions of matter, was carried out by Carey (1992), who presented 4-, 6-, 10-, and 12-year-olds, as well as adults, with three tasks related to the repeated halving of a piece of metal. Subjects were asked to judge whether the increasingly small pieces of metal had weight and took up space. Carey reported that about half of the children between the ages of 6 and 12, almost all the 12-year-olds, and all the adults maintained that solid substances are continuously divisible and that an arbitrarily small piece of substance still occupies a minuscule amount of space. Carey argued that students perceive material objects as infinitely divisible. We, however, attribute her findings, which are similar to ours, to the effect of the intuitive rule "Everything can be divided."

Response Patterns: Line Segment and Copper Wire

The analysis of students' response patterns to the previously described pair of tasks (the line-segment and the copper-wire problems) reveals that only about a third of the students in the upper grades came up with a correct response (i.e., a judgment assuming infinity in the line-segment task and a judgment assuming finity in the copper-wire task). The majority of the students at all grade levels gave the same (i.e., concordant) response to both tasks: either that the process of division is endless (the infinity pattern) or that the process will come to an end (the finity pattern). The frequency of the response pattern assuming infinity increased with grade level. Furthermore, almost all the students who showed a concordant response pattern also gave the same justification for their answers to both problems. Most students who showed the infinity response pattern argued that "it is always possible to divide by 2." Some students explicitly referred to the apparent concordance of these problems: "The process of dividing the line segment will never end, and this is exactly as with the copper wire; it is the same principle."

Closer examination of our data reveals that in the lower grades the majority of students who showed a concordant response pattern to the two tasks assumed finity. Starting in grade 9, however, a substantial number of students assumed infinity in both these tasks. The fact that a relatively large number of students exhibited a concordant response pattern assuming infinity supports our assertion that students tend to perceive repeated halving processes as endless, regardless of the nature of the object. Further support to this assertion comes from subsequent studies in which students were presented with similar tasks related to other mathematical and material objects (e.g., a geometric cube and a tin box).

Younger students' responses to the repeated halving problems— namely, their regarding both mathematical and physical repeated halving processes as finite—is in line with Piaget's observation about the early development of the idea of continuity. Piaget and Inhelder (1963), in their studies of the idea of points and the idea of continuity, presented children aged 4 to 15 with tasks related to repeated halving of some geometric figures (line segments, squares, circles, triangles, etc.) and analyzed their responses to questions about how far this process could continue. They identified several stages. At the first and second stages (up to age 7 or 8), the child can only make a very limited number of subdivisions when trying to break up a line segment or a surface. At the third stage (ages 7 or 8 to 11 or 12), the child is able to admit the possibility of a large, though not infinite, number of subdivisions. At the fourth stage, beginning around age 11 or 12, thought is liberated from the quasi-perceptual notions of the earlier stages, where concrete operations were hindered by the restrictive conditions of actual drawing and handling. Now subdivision can be conceived of as unlimited.

According to Piaget, at the level where thought becomes hypothetico-deductive, where operations are divested of their material content and begin to function solely in terms of their formal structure, the child can transcend the idea of visible subdivisions and perceptible points, and extend the mechanism of analysis and synthesis beyond any physical limit. It is this alone that facilitates the operational synthesis of continuity. At a certain stage the child becomes aware of the dynamics of the operation itself as a process of indefinite, abstract combination, subsequent to which subdivision and reassembly stop being simple additive operations applied to finite, material objects.

With regard to the comparison between material and geometric objects, Piaget argued:

> It is possible to trace out, step by step, a more or less parallel process of development for the idea of points and continuity and those dealing with atoms and physical objects in the child's conception of the external world. Thus, in watching a lump of sugar dissolve in a glass of water, he passes from the perception of visible though gradually diminishing particles to the idea of invisible grains, and finally to that of ultimately indivisible particles. Similarly, with a line or a figure, the child proceeds from the notion of parts that are separable but still perceptible, to that of invisible parts, smaller than but similar in principle to the former, and finally to the idea of its being reduced to ultimate indivisible particles. The only difference between these two processes is that to the child's way of thinking, physical points or atoms still possess surface and volume, whereas mathematical points tend to lose all extension. (Piaget & Inhelder, 1963, p. 126)

Piaget and Inhelder argued that students at the formal operational level discriminate between physical and mathematical objects. Our findings show that fewer than a third of the upper-grade students differentiated between the mathematical and the physical repeated halving tasks and gave correct responses (not necessarily accompanied with adequate justifications) to all of them. However, another response pattern was observed in these grades. About 40% of the students exhibited an response pattern assuming infinity to both pairs of repeated halving tasks. This suggests that children who have become aware that subdivision may continue endlessly tend to view repeated halving processes as endless, regardless of the constraints imposed by the nature of the objects (mathematical vs. physical). This perception was suggested by Hilbert (1925/1964), who claimed that viewing mathematical as well as physical objects as "ultimately divisible" is our first, naive impression of nature. However, our data suggest that this view is not a naive one: It develops with age and/or instruction.

Carrot. We have shown that repeated halving tasks elicit the use of the intuitive rule "Everything can be divided." So far we have dealt with repeated halving involving either mathematical or material objects.

In this section we refer to repeated halving involving biological objects. Biological objects consist of cells, which are the smallest biological units possessing the basic attributes of life (growth, reproduction, respiration, etc.). When this unit is disrupted, it loses its viability. Here, we examine the repeated halving of a carrot.

If you take a small piece of carrot, including at least one whole cell, and put it into a special growth solution, a whole carrot plant will grow out of it. In light of this biological behavior, we presented students in grades 7 to 11, who had studied cells in school, with the following task:

> Carol, who is very fond of carrots, decided to carry out the following experiment. She took a carrot, put it into a special growth solution, and was happy to discover that a whole carrot plant grew out of it. She was extremely impressed and decided to continue with her experiment. She made up her mind to take a whole carrot, cut it into half, put one-half in a growth solution, and cut the remaining part into halves. She would, again, put one-half in a growth solution and halve the remaining part, and so on.
>
> Is it possible to reach a stage at which the solution will not yield any carrot plant? Explain your answer.

A substantial number of students argued that this process will not come to a halt. Many simply explained that "it is always possible to divide the carrot by 2" or that "each piece of carrot can be halved." Others added that "a plant will always grow" or "it will grow infinitely." Some students further explained that "this process will never stop; it worked in all previous cases, and there is no reason for it to stop at a certain stage."

Only some of the students who correctly claimed that the process would come to an end related their response to the cellular level ("A carrot won't grow from a divided cell"). Some referred to the cell nucleus ("At a certain stage, the cell nucleus will be divided and after that, it won't grow") or to the lack of other parts of the plant that they conceived of as necessary for growth (e.g., seeds). Interestingly enough, few mentioned the molecular level ("The process will end when reaching the last molecule of the carrot"). The most frequent justifications assuming finity related to technical limitations ("The carrot will be too small to be cut"). Some argued that "the carrot will end."

Response Patterns: Line Segment, Copper Wire, and Carrot

It is interesting to look at the consistency in students' responses to tasks related to three different subject domains: mathematics, the physical sciences, and the biological sciences. The high percentages of concordant responses to a triplet of tasks—involving repeated halving of a line segment, a copper wire, and a carrot—show that students tend to respond in the same way to these tasks even though they relate to three different subject domains. Moreover, at all grade levels the frequencies of a response pattern assuming infinity are higher than the frequencies of both the correct (different) responses and the response pattern assuming finity.

Effects of Specific Properties of the Objects and the Nature of the Repeated Halving on Students' Responses

When one looks at students' responses to the tasks involving repeated halving described above, it becomes clear that the frequencies of responses assuming infinity varied somewhat with the specific properties of the objects. One observation is that, on average, infinity was assumed somewhat more frequently in the mathematical tasks than in the other tasks. Also, infinity was assumed slightly more often in the line-segment problem than in the geometric cube problem. These differences could possibly be due to the fact that one-dimensional objects involve only length and do not "have volume." The appearance of three-dimensional objects seems to somewhat undermine the rule "Everything can be divided."

It is reasonable to assume that if students are asked to make judgments about repeated halving of solids that appear to be discrete and are built of concrete, visible units (e.g., a grain of sand, a match), they would be less affected by the intuitive rule "Everything can be divided" than in cases where the solids appear to be continuous (e.g., a copper wire, a tin box).

To test this prediction, we presented seventh- to eleventh-graders with the following problems involving sand and matches:

1. Consider a bucket full of sand. Pour half of it out. Again, pour out half of the sand left in the bucket. Continue in the same way, each time pouring out half of the remaining sand. Will this process come to an end? Explain your answer.
2. In a game, each of two players has to put a number of matches on a square gameboard. The rules of the game are: The first player puts any number of matches on one square. The second player has to put, on another square, half the number of matches of the first player. Each player, alternately, puts exactly half the amount of matches of the previous stage in another square. Dan and Ron played this game. Dan put down 32 matches, Ron continued by putting down 16 matches, and so on. Will this game come to an end? Explain your answer.

Surprisingly, a substantial number of students in grades 7 to 11 (about a third) argued that the subdivision of sand and matches will never stop, because "one could always continue dividing." We expected that in this context practically all students would argue that the processes would come to an end. Such, however, was not the case. The non-negligible percentages of responses to these tasks that assumed infinity is an indication of the coercive effect of the intuitive rule "Everything can be divided" on students' responses.

Material objects can also differ in their state of matter. Information about the effect of this variable on students' responses was obtained by analyzing the responses of students in grades 7 to 10 to repeated halving processes involving three substances in different states: a tin box, water in a cup, and iodine gas in a container. We chose the iodine because it is colored (violet) and thus visible, like the other two substances. Our data indicate that there were only minor differences between the rates of responses assuming infinity to these three tasks (see Table 3.1).

The material objects presented so far were visible. We predicted that when asked about the finite/infinite nature of repeated halving processes involving nonvisible substances (e.g., oxygen gas), the percentages of responses assuming infinity would be higher, because in such cases no perceptual clues could inhibit the use of the intuitive rule. To test this prediction, we presented students in grades 7 to 10 with two tasks related to repeated halving of gases: iodine (a violet gas) and oxygen (a colorless gas).

Our data confirm that visibility does affect students' responses to repeated halving. At each of these grade levels, the percentages of responses assuming infinity as regards oxygen were higher than those as regards iodine. Notably, about 50% of the students in the upper grades gave responses assuming infinity to the oxygen task. Most students who gave responses assuming infinity to both these tasks explained that "everything can be divided by two" or that "there is always half of half." Justifications for re-

Table 3.1 Distribution, by Grade, of Responses Assuming Infinity to Different States of Matter (in %)

Task	Grade			
	7	8	9	10
Tin box	27	36	46	37
Water	16	28	38	38
Iodine	23	28	33	31

sponses assuming infinity to the oxygen task, unlike to the iodine task, included such comments as that "it is impossible to see it."

Notably, some students referred to the tendency of the oxygen to spread and fill up the entire container. For instance, Miriam, a tenth-grader, explained that "the oxygen will always spread in the container, and therefore it is always possible to take out half of it." Such responses were also given, although to a lesser extent, in regard to the iodine. Some students argued that "when taking out half of the oxygen, air enters into the container, and oxygen and air are mixed together."

So far, we have examined students' responses to repeated halving of various objects. We have shown that a substantial number of students gave responses assuming infinity to these tasks, involving mathematical, material, and biological objects, invoking the intuitive rule "Everything can be divided." We have also shown that the responses assuming infinity increased with grade level.

We further examined the effects of four factors on students' responses: dimensions, discrete appearance, state of matter, and visibility. Three of these factors had some effect on students' responses: dimension, discrete appearance, and visibility.

We were curious to examine the effect of still another factor—the specific nature of the repeated halving—on students' responses. In all previous tasks, students were faced with one type of repeated halving—namely, halving the object, taking one-half, halving it, and so on. Malleability, however, involves halving the thickness of a piece of metal while conserving its total amount. This process terminates when the atomic level is reached.

We presented students in grades 9 to 11 with the following task:

> The sophisticated robot "Malleable" works on a piece of metal.
> In each operation, the robot flattens a piece of copper to half its
> original thickness. The robot starts operating on a given piece of
> metal, reducing its thickness by two. Then, again, the robot re-
> duces the thickness of the same piece of metal by two. The pro-
> cess continues in the same way.
> Will this process come to an end? Explain your answer.

Our data show that the subjects responded to this task in much the same way as they did to the task concerning the repeated halving of solid objects (40%, 30%, and 57% in grades 9, 10, and 11, respectively). Most of the students claimed the flattening process would be endless, justifying their answers by arguments in line with the intuitive rule "Everything can be divided." Most of those who correctly argued that the process comes to an end used technical, macroscopic explanations.

In a related study (Ben-Zvi, Eylon, & Silberstein, 1986), high school students were asked whether an atom of copper is malleable. It was found that many students believed that an isolated atom of copper has the same properties as a piece of copper and that both the atom and the piece of metal are malleable. Students' claims that an atom of copper is malleable could be viewed as a manifestation of the intuitive rule "Everything can be divided."

Another type of task involves decomposition of radioactive materials. Consider the following task:

> Radioactive materials are substances that decompose and emit radioactive radiation. Half the life of a radioactive substance is defined by the time it takes for half the amount of the radioactive substance to decompose.
>
> Let's consider a sample of phosphorus that contains some radioactive phosphorus. Its half-life is 14 days, that is, half of the radioactive phosphorus decomposes in 14 days. Half the remaining radioactive phosphorus decomposes in the next 14 days, and so on. Is it possible to reach a stage at which no radioactive phosphorus at all will be found in the phosphorus sample? Explain your answer.

The rate of the decomposition process depends on the amount of the radioactive material, and it will continue until one atom of radioactive phosphorus is left. Seventh- to eleventh-grade students' responses to this task were similar to those related to the repeated halving of substances and to malleability. Again, common justifications for responses assuming infinity were of the type "The process will always continue because everything has a half" and "There is always half of a half." Some students referred to the specific nature of the substance, explaining that "there will always remain some radioactive material in the phosphorus" or "the radiation will continue forever." Thus, it seems that the nature of the substance undergoing repeated halving has no effect on students' responses.

DECREASING SERIES

In this section we present students' responses to decreasing-series tasks involving mathematical, material, and biological objects. The high percentages of responses assuming infinity to these tasks (around 70% in the upper grades) indicate the strong effect of the intuitive rule "Everything can be divided" on students' responses.

Number. A typical question, relating to series, is:

> Consider the number 1, divide it by 2, divide the obtained num-
> ber by 2, continue dividing the obtained numbers in the same
> way. Will this process of division come to an end? Will zero be
> reached?

This question featured in various studies conducted by us and by other researchers (e.g., Tall, 1981; Tirosh, 1985; Tirosh & Stavy, 1996). These studies consistently reported that the vast majority (at least 90%) of high school
students knew that this process is endless, because "any number can be
divided by 2." Falk, Gassner, Ben-Zoor, and Ben-Simon (1986) gave young
children (kindergarten to seventh grade) a somewhat similar problem, presented in a format of a two-player game (the researcher and a child):

> Each of us should say a number. The one whose number is
> smaller will win. Would you like to be the first or the second?

This game was played in several versions, in one of which children were
allowed to use only positive numbers, including fractions. Falk and colleagues (1986) found that from grade 3 on, the majority of the students
chose to be the second player. In her paper, she quoted Yoram (grade 5): "I
think we will never reach zero, we'll only get closer to it each time; even
though the interval [between zero and one] looks small, it includes all the
numbers in the world, because each number you can turn into 1 divided by
the number."

Shandy.

> The popular drink shandy is a mixture of equal amounts of beer
> and lemon soda. Dana went with her friends to a bar and all of
> them ordered shandy. Dana tasted the shandy and felt it was too
> bitter. She poured out half of the shandy, filled the half-emptied
> cup with lemon soda, and mixed thoroughly with the remaining
> drink. She tasted the mixture, and it was still too bitter. Therefore
> she again poured out half of the diluted shandy, added lemon
> soda, mixing everything thoroughly. She repeated this process
> again and again.
>   Is it possible that at a certain stage she will have pure lemon
> soda, with no beer? Explain your answer.

The concentration of beer in the shandy could be described by the series
1/2, 1/4, 1/8, etc. However, at a certain stage, due to the particulate nature

of matter, it is possible that no molecules of beer will be left in the cup. The vast majority of the students (83%, 83%, and 79% in grades 9, 10, and 11, respectively) argued that "beer will always remain in the cup." Typical justifications were that "there is always half of the beer" and that "the beer and the lemon soda are mixed together, and therefore there will always remain beer in the cup." Most students assuming finity simply stated that "the amount of beer is finite, and eventually all of it will be poured out." Only few referred to "particles" or "molecules" of beer.

In this case, the beer is spread throughout the entire cup and therefore is halved along with the solvent. Thus, an impression may be created that both beer and lemon soda will always be present in the cup. The characteristics of this serial dilution task possibly trigger responses assuming infinity.

Sugarwater.

> A teaspoon of sugar is put into a cup of water and stirred well into it. Half of the sugarwater is poured out, and half a cup of water is added to the cup and is mixed thoroughly with the remaining sugarwater. This is done again: Half of the sugarwater is poured out, half a cup of water is added, and so forth. This process is repeated. Is it possible that there is a stage at which no sugar at all will be found in the cup? Explain your answer.

This problem refers to decreasing concentrations of sugar in solutions. Due to the particulate nature of matter, after a large number of dilutions, the resulting solution might have a zero concentration of sugar.

This problem was presented to students in grades 7 to 11. Again, the percentages of responses assuming infinity were high (around 60% at each of the grade levels). Many students claimed that the amount of sugar would become smaller and smaller but never reach zero because "Everything can be divided." Some explained that the dissolved sugar could not disappear because "it mixes with water and spreads in it, and only half of both are poured out each time." Similar responses were provided by students to essentially the same task, this one involving serial dilution of "red raspberry juice."

Salt and sugar. The serial dilution tasks described above involved at least one liquid (the solvent). We presented students with the following analogous task involving a mixture of two solids:

> Naughty John put a tablespoon of salt into a bowl of sugar and mixed it well into the sugar. Then he regretted his action. He

poured out half of the salt–sugar mixture, filled the bowl up with sugar, and stirred it in thoroughly with the remaining mixture. He tasted the mixture and could still taste the salt. Therefore he repeated the action of pouring out half of the salt–sugar mixture, adding sugar, mixing everything thoroughly. He repeated this process again and again.

Is it possible to reach a stage at which no salt at all will be present in the bowl? Explain your answer.

The method used by John could eventually lead to separating the salt out of the sugar. In fact, this is a process of serial dilution of salt. Yet, although this process involves substances that appear to be discrete, the vast majority of the students (around 80% in the upper grades) argued that "salt will always remain in the sugar." Common justifications were: "You can always halve a half"; "Salt and sugar are mixed, they will pour together, and half the salt will always be poured out with half of the sugar, and therefore salt will always be left"; and "Salt could not disappear."

The rates of responses assuming infinity in the shandy and the salt–sugar problems are somewhat higher than those of the responses to the sugarwater-solution and the raspberry-juice tasks. Possibly, the visual similarity of the lemon soda and beer and of the salt and sugar in these tasks supports the use of the intuitive rule.

Yeast. In the previous section, we showed that the intuitive rule "Everything can be divided" is manifested in students' responses to repeated halving of biological objects. Here we examine students' responses to a serial-dilution task involving biological objects. Serial dilution is often used to estimate the number of cells in a given sample (e.g., bacteria, blood cells). We presented ninth- to eleventh-graders with the following task involving serial dilution of a yeast suspension:

Amy's mother intended to prepare a yeast cake. She mixed a certain amount of yeast with water. Amy thought that her mother used too much yeast. She poured out half of the mixture, filled the cup with water, and stirred well. Still, she thought that there was too much yeast and decided to repeat the process: She poured out half of the mixture, added water, and mixed again. She repeated the process again and again.

Is it possible that she reaches a stage when there will only be pure water, with no yeast, left in the cup? Explain your answer.

Most students at all grade levels argued that it is impossible to reach a stage at which no yeast will be left (53%, 63%, and 70% in grades 9, 10, and 11, respectively). Most students explained that "everything can be halved" or that "you can always halve a half." Some argued that "the yeast is mixed/dissolved/absorbed in the water and at each stage half of it will be left." Some mentioned the possibility that yeast will grow and reproduce during the course of this process.

Very few students who chose a response assuming finity correctly claimed that "the process will continue until the last yeast cell." Some of the other students who chose a response assuming finity referred to "molecules, atoms, grains." Most responses assuming finity were justified by the claim that "the amount of yeast is finite," or that "the concentration of yeast will decrease until it reaches zero," or that "eventually, all the yeast will pour out."

The relatively high percentages of incorrect responses assuming infinity could be interpreted as an instance of the use of the rule "Everything can be divided." Our data indicate that even students who knew that a cell is the basic unit of the living organism provided responses assuming infinity to this task (Cohen, 1997).

SOME QUESTIONS ABOUT THE USE OF THIS RULE

Many tasks involving successive division were presented in the previous two sections. All these tasks have some common features: Each of them describes a process of successive division and asks the student to determine whether it will come to an end. The correct response depends on the nature of the object: The process is infinite when the object in question is mathematical and finite when it is material or biological. Unexpectedly, the percentages of students from grade 9 and up who gave responses assuming infinity to the material and biological tasks were relatively high. These relatively high rates of incorrect responses could be interpreted as instances of the use of the rule "Everything can be divided."

The frequency of responses assuming infinity varied with the type of process. Clearly, more students gave responses assuming infinity to the decreasing-series tasks than to the repeated-halving ones. These differences could be attributed to the fact that in the repeated-halving tasks, unlike in the decreasing-series tasks, the pieces involved become smaller and smaller. Thus, students tended to argue that the process comes to an end when the pieces become too small to be halved. Decreasing-series tasks, however, do not involve visible diminution of the divided objects, and this possibly encourages the application of the rule.

One might argue that responses assuming infinity to the tasks involving successive division of material and biological objects result from students' perception of matter and living organisms as continuous and their lack of knowledge of the particulate theory of matter and of the cellular structure of living organisms. However, many students who exhibited an adequate knowledge of these topics in other tasks still provided responses assuming infinity to subdivision tasks (Cohen, 1997; Egozi, 1993). Thus, it seems that tasks involving successive division activate the rule "Everything can be divided," a rule that strongly competes with formal knowledge.

Why Do We Call "Everything Can Be Divided" an Intuitive Rule?

We suggest that this response has the status of a rule because it is accompanied by adverbs such as *everything, always, never,* etc. This rule is intuitive: It was observed that the response "Everything can be divided" is taken as self-evident (subjects perceived their statements based on this rule to be true without need for further justification) and is used with great confidence and perseverance (it persists in spite of formal learning about the particulate nature of matter and about the cellular structure of living organisms). Moreover, this rule has attributes of globality (subjects tend to apply it to all objects) and coerciveness (alternatives are excluded as unacceptable).

What Is the Origin of This Intuitive Rule?

"Everything can be divided" is an intuitive rule that is triggered by situations of successive division. We suggest that this rule derives from the natural tendency of our cognitive system to extrapolate. In this case, the extrapolation is from a visible stage in the process of subdividing a given object, to the next stage, and then to the next stage, and so on. Beginning at a certain age, subjects see no reason to argue that at a certain stage this extrapolation will not be valid anymore. Reference to this was made by Poincaré (1906, quoted in Fischbein, 1987), who argued that "it is the affirmation of the power of the spirit which feels itself capable of conceiving the infinite repetition of the same act if this act has once been possible" (p. 52). In the case of the intuitive rule "Everything can be divided," the repeated act is that of division.

How Stable Is This Rule?

To explore this issue, we presented students in grades 7 to 12 with two hypothetical, contradictory student responses to various successive-division tasks involving mathematical and material objects (Tirosh, Stavy, & Cohen,

1998). One response suggests that the described process of successive division will come to an end when reaching a small piece/a basic unit. This judgment is correct for tasks involving material objects. The second hypothetical student response, in line with the rule "Everything can be divided," suggests that the process is endless. This judgment is correct when mathematical objects are considered. The students were asked to choose between the two alternatives in their responses to the tasks.

This study included two phases.

Phase I: Responses to Subdivision Problems

The problems were as follows:

Repeated-halving tasks.

1. Consider a rectangle. Divide it into two equal rectangles. Divide one of these rectangles into two equal rectangles. Continue dividing in the same way. Will this process come to an end? Yes/ No. Explain your answer.
2. Consider a rectangular piece of aluminum foil. Divide it into two equal parts. Divide one-half into two equal parts. Continue dividing in the same way. Will this process come to an end? Yes/ No. Explain your answer.

Decreasing-series tasks.

3. Consider the series: 1, 1/2, 1/4, 1/8, 1/16, 1/32, 1/64, 1/128 . . .
   In this series, each number is half the previous one. Will this process of dividing the numbers come to an end? Yes/ No. Explain your answer.
4. A teaspoon of sugar is put into a cup of water and stirred well into it. Half of the sugarwater is poured out, half a cup of plain water is added to the cup and is mixed thoroughly with the remaining sugarwater. This process is executed again: Half of the sugarwater is poured out, half a cup of water is added, and so forth. This process is repeated.
   Is it possible to reach a stage at which no sugar at all will be found in the cup? Yes/No. Explain your answer.

Half the students at each grade level were first given the tasks related to mathematical objects (tasks 1 and 3) on one sheet of paper. The problems related to material objects (tasks 2 and 4) were then provided on a different sheet of paper. The other half of the participants received the tasks in the reversed order. The questionnaire was administered during a regular, general class period (neither mathematics nor science class).

Phase II: Intervention

This questionnaire repeated the four tasks included in phase I, but in this phase each task was followed by two short statements presented as two hypothetical, contradictory student responses to the task. Subjects were asked to determine which, if any, of these written statements were correct and to justify their answer.

For the task concerning repeated halving of the rectangle (task 1), for instance, the two following statements were given as hypothetical student responses:

> *Arnold*: This process will not end, because every geometric object can be divided by 2.
>
> *Nancy*: The process will come to an end, because eventually a small rectangle, which cannot be further divided, will be reached.

For the task about the repeated halving of the rectangular piece of aluminum foil (task 2), the following statements were provided:

> *Dan*: This process will not end, because every piece of aluminum foil can be divided by 2.
>
> *Nora*: The process will come to an end, because eventually an atom, which cannot be divided anymore, will be reached.

Clearly, one of the hypothetical student responses to each task would contradict the initial response of the student responding to the problem. The student was therefore faced with a situation that could challenge his or her confidence in that initial response and demand consideration and reevaluation of that response. Our data show that the vast majority of the subjects who gave responses assuming infinity to each of the four tasks in phase I gave the same responses to these tasks in phase II. This shows that the intuitive rule "Everything can be divided" is very stable and was not affected by the hypothetical contradictory responses to the tasks.

4

Toward a Theory of Intuitive Rules

In the first three chapters, we presented ample examples of typical inappropriate responses of variously aged students to a wide variety of mathematics and science tasks. We designed some of these tasks specifically, while others are well known. Some were presented previously by other researchers (e.g., Piaget, 1952/1965), some were listed in reviews and bibliographies describing students' alternative conceptions (e.g., Carmicheal et al., 1990; Confrey, 1990; Driver et al., 1985; Gilbert & Watts, 1983; Pfundt & Duit, 1994), and some were presented at scientific meetings (Novak, 1983, 1987).

We were surprised to find out that students gave the same type of response to scientifically unrelated tasks. In Chapter 1 we described many tasks to which the same inappropriate response was "More A–More B," in Chapter 2 we looked at the inappropriate response "Same A–Same B," and in Chapter 3 we examined the inappropriate response "Everything can be divided." The fact that students gave the same type of response to scientifically unrelated tasks raised our curiosity. We asked ourselves: What do tasks that elicit the same type of response have in common?

All tasks that elicited the response "More A–More B" were comparison tasks that described two objects differing in a certain salient quantity, A ($A_1 > A_2$). Students were then asked to compare the two objects with respect to another quantity, B (B_1 is not larger than B_2, that is, $B_1 = B_2$ or $B_1 < B_2$). Similarly, tasks that evoked the response "Same A–Same B" were comparison tasks in which two objects, equal in a certain quantity, A, were described ($A_1 = A_2$). The students were asked to compare B_1 and B_2 ($B_1 \neq B_2$). The tasks that elicited the response "Everything can be divided" were all successive-division tasks in which students were asked to determine whether the repeated subdivision of an object would come to a halt.

The commonalties in the tasks that elicited *the same type of response* were in the external features of the tasks, not in their scientific content. We have shown that students' responses to mathematics and science tasks do not necessarily accord with scientific frameworks and concepts. Students' responses are often determined by certain task features that activate related, specific intuitive rules.

THEORETICAL APPROACHES TO STUDENTS' ALTERNATIVE REASONING AND CONCEPTIONS

Our approach to students' responses substantially departs from mainstream research on students' incorrect responses in the mathematics and science education communities. One type of such mainstream research attempts to identify the forms of reasoning required to provide correct responses to given tasks, arguing that incorrect responses result from lack of required cognitive schemes (e.g., Flavell, 1963; Lawson, 1995; Piaget, 1969; Piaget & Inhelder, 1974; Shayer & Adey, 1981). This influential approach accounts for and predicts many incorrect responses that students of particular ages provide on given tasks. It does not, however, account for the variability in students' responses to different tasks that, according to these theories, demand the very same logical schemes (e.g., the phenomenon of horizontal decalage).

Another main line of research on students' inappropriate responses to mathematics and scientific tasks has been the alternative-conception paradigm (e.g., Carey, 1985; Driver, 1994; McClosky, 1983a, 1983b; Novak & Gowin, 1984; Osborne & Freyberg, 1985; Tall & Vinner, 1981; Thijs & van den Berg, 1995; Vosniadou & Brewer, 1987). This approach aimed at detailed descriptions of certain particular alternative conceptions, where the child takes an active, constructive role in the knowledge-acquisition process and brings to the learning situations alternative, internally coherent, robust, and persistent conceptions. Yet there is evidence that students tend to respond inconsistently to tasks related to the very same mathematical or scientific concept (Clough & Driver, 1986; diSessa, 1983; Noss & Hoyles, 1996; Nunes, Schliemann, & Carraher, 1993; Smith, diSessa, & Roschelle, 1993; Svensson, 1989; Tirosh, 1990; Tytler, 1998a, 1998b). This evidence challenges the alternative-conception paradigm.

Fischbein (1987) suggested that many students' science and mathematics conceptions as evidenced in their responses are intuitive, pointing to different primary and secondary intuitions in different domains of scientific and mathematical content. We mentioned before that each of the rules we suggested has the characteristics of intuitive reasoning. Our intuitive rules, however, are logical, intuitive schemes activated by specific external features of the tasks; they are not embedded within a specific content domain.

Several researchers have observed some shared features in students' responses to different physics tasks, leading them to suggest underlying common cores of these responses. Thus, Andersson (1986) analyzed children's responses to a large group of tasks related to temperature and heat, electricity, optics, and mechanics. He identified a common core in them, which he called the *experiential gestalt of causation*, and posited that this gestalt consists of an agent, instrument, and object. The agent, directly with his or her own body or indirectly with the help of an instrument, affects the object. Through repeated testing and investigating in the world, this experiential gestalt is reinforced, and the child discovers quantitative relationships between causes and effects: The greater the effort he or she makes, the greater the effect on the object. This response is in accordance with the first intuitive rule, "More A–More B," and could be regarded as an instance of it.

Another attempt to find commonalties in students' responses in different physics content areas was made by Gutierrez and Ogborn (1992). They proposed a causal model for analyzing students' alternative conceptions, drawing on de Kleer and Brown's (1983, 1984) model. Gutierrez and Ogborn's model purports to provide an explanation for the possible causal structure of children's and adults' spontaneous reasoning about the physical world. This model has five main qualitative notions: locality (cause near effect), asymmetry (cause precedes effect), productivity (effect produced by cause), constancy (cause always has effect), and uniqueness (same cause–same effect). This model describes the forms, not the content, of causal reasoning. Subsequently, Gutierrez and Ogborn used this framework for the analysis of students' understanding of forces and motions. Some of their qualitative notions are in line with the intuitive rules, but, once again, they relate to physical concepts only.

A third attempt to analyze students' reasoning in science was made by Viennot (1985), who looked for a formulation of causal reasoning that would be broad enough to cover many kinds of physical systems. She suggested that students tended to answer as if they had in mind a "conceptual structure" or "a way of reasoning" described by "*if* (set of situations) *then* (features of response)." An example of this can be found in Engle (1982) and Sere (1982), who reported that in a situation involving vessels containing air under pressure with no movement, students commonly argued that the air does not push and that there is no pressure. Viennot concluded that these students responded as if they had in mind the rule "Pressure only has meaning *if* there is a displacement." In this work, the set of situations that triggers a certain response was not defined.

These last three groups of researchers attempted to explain, in causal terms, students' reasoning with regard to physics tasks. Our intuitive rules apply to a much wider scope, including mathematics, physics, biology, and chemistry tasks and perhaps other domains as well.

Reference to the effects of the surface features of the tasks on students' responses can be found in research involving the novice–expert shift (e.g., Chi, Feltovich, & Glaser, 1981; Larkin & Rainhard, 1984). Studies within this paradigm indicate that inexperienced solvers tend to mentally represent a given problem according to surface features, whereas experienced solvers refer to scientific concepts and principles. Our approach also emphasizes the role that external features play in determining students' responses to given tasks. We, however, analyzed the specific task features that activate related, specific intuitive rules, resulting in specific responses.

SOME QUESTIONS ABOUT THE INTUITIVE RULES THEORY

Our interpretation of students' incorrect responses could be regarded as a theory. This theory has two main strengths: (1) It accounts for many of the observed incorrect responses to science and mathematics tasks, and (2) it has a strong predictive power; that is, when a certain task is described, it is possible to predict students' responses to this task on the basis of the specific external features of the task and the relevant intuitive rule.

The essential claim of the intuitive rules theory is that human responses are determined mainly by irrelevant external features of the tasks, not by related concepts and ideas. That human responses should rely mainly on irrelevant external factors, rather than on the accepted scientific framework or on alternative conceptions related to the specific concept, is hard to accept. This book, therefore, provides many examples, in the hope that they will lead the reader to the inevitable realization that, indeed, specific external features of given tasks activate intuitive rules and determine our responses.

Some questions that could be raised regarding the intuitive rules theory include the following.

How Can We Explain the Fact That the Very Same Task Sometimes Triggers the Use of One Intuitive Rule While Activating Another Intuitive Rule at Other Times?

Indeed, the data show that the same task might result in different responses. A closer examination reveals that in both the comparison and the subdivision tasks, younger students tend to come up with one type of response (i.e., More A–More B; Everything comes to an end), whereas older students give another type of response (Same A–Same B; Everything can be divided). In both cases, the responses of the younger students seem to be activated by immediate, concrete, and perceptual features of the task (e.g., the perceptual differences between the two compared objects in quantity A; the technical limitations imposed on the subdivision process by the concrete nature of the object). Older students can ignore immediate perceptual cues and applied logical considerations. Yet, as shown earlier, the application of some of these logical considerations is overgeneralized, yielding incorrect responses of the type "Same A–Same B" or "Everything can be divided."

Here our approach differs significantly from that of Piaget. While Piaget assumed that the acquisition of a certain logical scheme presupposes controlled use of it, we have shown this is not the case. The application of newly acquired schemes is often overgeneralized. For instance, the fact that a child provides a correct conservation response to a given task could be an instance of the use of the rule "Same A–Same B," not necessarily a controlled use of the conservation scheme.

Can We Explain All Incorrect Responses as Resulting from These Intuitive Rules?

We are not arguing that *all* incorrect responses to *all* tasks can be interpreted as resulting from the application of these three intuitive rules. First, some incorrect responses to certain tasks seem to be related to specific contents and mental representations. For instance, responses to questions such as What is a triangle? What is a solid? Is a plant a living organism? will probably not be affected by the application of the intuitive rules (these tasks are neither comparison nor subdivision tasks). Second, so far we have identified three intuitive rules: "More A–More B," "Same A–Same B," and "Everything can be divided." This does not imply that there are no other intuitive rules that are activated in other types of tasks. We are currently engaged in the exploration of other possible intuitive rules; for instance, a possible rule affecting inferences is "If A, then B–If not A, then not B."

Do These Rules Apply Only to Mathematics and Science Education?

The three intuitive rules we have identified so far allow the prediction of students' responses to many comparison and subdivision tasks. In this book, we have restricted ourselves to mathematical, physical, and biological tasks. There is, however, evidence that these intuitive rules affect our responses in other domains as well. For instance, speaking on the phone with overseas friends or colleagues often automatically results in raising one's voice. A possible cause of this behavior is the intuitive rule "More A (distance)–More B (voice level)." Similarly, a very well known phenomenon involving choirs is that when a conductor requests the choir to slow the rhythm, the singers often automatically respond by lowering their voices as well. Other examples could be found in other domains as well.

How Do We Overcome the Effect of the Intuitive Rules?

We suggest that with age and/or instruction, schemes, formal rules, and bodies of knowledge related to specific content areas are developed and reinforced. Consequently, in respect to these content areas, the relevant intuitive rule loses its power in the face of competing knowledge. It is also possible that with age and/or instruction, children become aware of the need to examine their initial responses, to consider other factors that might be relevant to the task, and to avoid conflicting arguments. Thus, learners may gradually become aware of the boundaries within which a given intuitive rule is applicable.

We have argued that although students cease to use a given rule in certain instances at certain ages, they never stop using it altogether and it continues to dominate in various other situations. We have given evidence of this in previous chapters. In Chapter 1, for instance, we demonstrated that university students still apply the rule "More A–More B" in free-fall tasks, arguing that "the heavier–the faster." We have also shown that older children and adults continue using the intuitive rules even after formal, related instruction.

What Is the Origin of These Intuitive Rules?

We claim that the intuitive rules are expressions of the natural tendency of our cognitive system to extrapolate. We argued earlier that the origin of two intuitive rules that relate to comparison tasks is the extrapolation from a given relationship between two systems with regard to a certain quantity, A, to the relationship between these two systems in respect to another quantity, B. In the case of the intuitive rule "More A–More B," the response $B_1 > B_2$ is probably extrapolated from immediate perceptual differences in quantity A (e.g., length, mass) or from salient differences between symbols associated with perceptual images of this quantity (e.g., numbers). Similarly, in the case of the rule "Same A–Same B," the response $B_1 = B_2$ is extrapolated from explicitly given or logically derived information about the equality in quantity A. The intuitive rule "Everything can be divided" is a direct consequence of the natural tendency of our cognitive system to extrapolate. Here the extrapolation is from a given stage to the next one.

The general tendency to extrapolate is an extremely valuable learning resource. For instance, a child sees the sun rising day after day and concludes, by extrapolation, that it will rise tomorrow, and the day after tomorrow, and so forth. A primary aim of mathematics and science education is to encourage students to extrapolate and transfer knowledge of principles, concepts, and skills from one specific instance to others. A well-known concern, often discussed in the mathematics and science literature, is the inefficiency of the educational system in this respect. Many studies have shown that students are not making such desired connections (e.g., Noss & Hoyles, 1996). In this book we have shown that students do extrapolate from the known to the unknown but that this extrapolation is based not on the essential features of the content domain but rather on external features. Such extrapolations are not desirable.

This situation causes a dilemma to mathematics and science education. On the one hand, extrapolation from one given situation to another, when based on scientific principles, is to be encouraged. On the other hand, natural extrapolations based on external features (even in cases where they coincide with scientific principles) should be critically examined. This dilemma obviously poses substantial challenges to mathematics and science education. We discuss this and other educational implications of the theory of intuitive rules in the final chapter.

5

Using Knowledge About Intuitive Rules: Educational Implications

In the previous chapters, we introduced a theory that accounts for many students' incorrect responses in science and mathematics. We have shown that this theory has predictive power. Once we are acquainted with the theory of intuitive rules, it is quite natural to raise the following questions:

> What are the educational implications of this theory? How can we use it to improve science and mathematics education?

A first, immediate response to these questions is: Teachers of mathematics and science should become aware of the role of intuitive rules in students' thinking. They should take this knowledge into consideration when planning instruction. This response, however, immediately raises related questions:

> How can teachers use their knowledge about intuitive rules to improve science and mathematics education? What can they do?

We have decided to tackle this issue in several ways. First, we suggest some teaching methods that aim to help students overcome the effects of the intuitive rules. Second, we describe how some of our colleagues, who became acquainted with the intuitive rules theory, have used this knowledge in mathematics and science education.

OVERCOMING THE EFFECTS OF THE INTUITIVE RULES: GENERAL AND SPECIFIC TEACHING STRATEGIES

A general objective of science and mathematics education is to encourage students' critical thinking (e.g., National Council of Teachers of Mathematics, 1989). In light of the theory of intuitive rules, which essentially claims that students' responses to given tasks often rely on external, irrelevant features, the importance of encouraging critical thinking is evident. Students should be encouraged not to rely on external features of the tasks, but to critically examine their responses. They should be encouraged to regularly ask themselves questions such as: What are the boundaries within which my response is valid? (Is it valid for different types of numbers? Is it valid under all conditions?) Does it fit in with other things I know? (For instance, with my knowledge about geometric entities, with my knowledge about the particulate nature of matter?) Encouraging students to critically examine their own responses should, however, be done in a careful, delicate manner, without thereby discouraging basic thinking mechanisms (e.g., generalization and extrapolation).

On a more specific level, we discuss teaching methods that can be used in specific situations within specific content domains. We would suggest the use of three teaching approaches: teaching by analogy, conflict teaching, and attention to relevant variables.

Teaching by Analogy

In teaching by analogy, students are first presented with an "anchoring task" in whose formulation the irrelevant features that trigger the use of a given intuitive rule are absent (this anchoring task usually elicits a correct response). Later on, students are presented with a series of essentially similar "bridging tasks" in which the irrelevant features known to elicit the intuitive rule are progressively more evident. Finally a "target task," known to strongly suggest the intuitive rule, is introduced (a detailed description of the teaching by analogy approach is given in Clement, 1993).

Such a sequence of instruction was proven to be effective in helping students overcome the effect of the intuitive rule "More A–More B" in the context of comparing vertical angles (Tsamir, 1997). In Chapter 1, we presented students' responses to tasks involving comparison of vertical angles. We have shown that when vertical angles with arms of equal length were presented, practically all students at all grade levels correctly responded that the angles were equal. However, when the angles showed arms of different lengths, the percentages of students who responded that these angles were equal were substantially lower than in the previous task. A substantial number of students argued that angle β was larger. This claim was accompanied by the explanation that "β is larger because its lines are longer." This explanation is in line with the intuitive rule "More A–More B."

In teaching by analogy, the drawing of vertical angles with arms of equal length was used as the anchoring task, and a mixed-typed representation served as the bridging task. The mixed-typed representation was presented as shown in Figure 5.1, and then the page was rotated by 90°, in front of the students, to obtain a representation of vertical angles with unequal arms—the target task. This series of tasks, starting with an anchoring one, through the bridging one, to the target task, significantly improved students' responses to the target task (Tsamir, 1997). Similar series of tasks, utilizing the predictive power of the intuitive rules, could be used in other content domains as well.

Figure 5.1 Vertical Angles: Different Representations

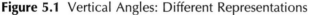
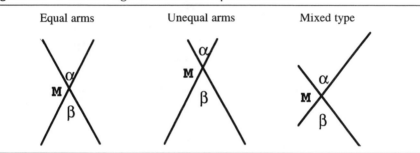

Conflict Teaching Approach

In the conflict teaching approach, students are first given a task known to elicit an incorrect response, and then they are presented with a situation that contradicts their initial response. Such a presentation may raise students' awareness of the inadequacy of their initial response (Piaget, 1980). Applied to intuitive rules, a conflict can be generated by first presenting students with a task known to forcefully trigger one of the intuitive rules, leading to incorrect response. Then contradiction may be created in several ways—for instance, by presenting students with contradictory concrete evidence; presenting them with a task that is essentially similar to the initial task but known to elicit a correct response; or confronting them with related formal knowledge (extreme cases).

Concrete Evidence

Consider, for instance, the task referring to the surface area and volume of two cylinders, which was presented in Chapter 2. It was reported that students tended to incorrectly claim that the volumes of two different cylinders made from identical rectangular sheets of paper are the same, applying the rule "Same A (area)–Same B (volume)." When students in grade 5 were asked to test their predictions by measuring the amount of lentils needed to fill each of the cylinders, they discovered that their initial prediction was incorrect and that the shorter cylinder contained more lentils than the taller one (Segal, in press). Subsequently, students tended to abandon their initial "Same A–Same B" response to this task and to similar tasks in favor of the correct one (the volume of the shorter cylinder is larger than that of the taller one).

Myers (1998) obtained similar results in respect to free-fall tasks. She presented students in grade 8 with two identical plastic boxes, one filled with small stones and the other empty. The two boxes were held at the same height above the ground, in the same manner. Students were asked to predict whether the boxes would hit the ground at the same time and, if not, which would hit the ground first (assuming that the boxes were dropped at the same instant). Myers found that about half of the participants incorrectly predicted that the heavier box would reach the ground first, because "the heavier–the faster." Then she dropped the two boxes in front of the students, asking them to describe what they saw. Later, a questionnaire was administered including essentially the same free-fall task, albeit with two balls, identical in size but different in weight. Practically all the students who had previously observed the two boxes hitting the ground at the same time responded correctly.

Different Representations

In the previous two cases, conflict was created between the students' initial incorrect predictions, in line with an intuitive rule, and contradictory concrete evidence. Conflict may also be generated by presenting students with two essentially similar tasks, the first known to activate an intuitive rule, resulting in an incorrect response, and the second known to trigger a correct response (Langer, 1969; Strauss, 1972). Students either recognize for themselves, or are encouraged to realize, that the two tasks are essentially similar but that their responses to the two tasks contradict each other. Students are then asked to reconsider their initial responses.

Tirosh and Tsamir (1996) used their knowledge about the effects of intuitive rules on students' responses to tasks involving comparison of infinite sets to improve their responses to such tasks. They first presented students with the following task:

Consider the two infinite sets:
{1, 2, 3, 4, . . . }
{1, 4, 9, 16, . . . }

Is the number of elements in these sets the same? If not, which set contains more elements? Why?

As expected, most students in grades 10 to 12 argued incorrectly, in line with the intuitive rule "More A–More B," that the set $\{1, 2, 3, 4, \ldots\}$ contained more elements because it contained all the elements in the set $\{1, 4, 9, 16, \ldots\}$ and some other elements as well. Then students were offered the same problem, presented in the following way:

Consider two infinite sets:
$$\{1, 2, 3, 4, \ldots\}$$
$$\{1^2, 2^2, 3^2, 4^2, \ldots\}$$
Is the number of elements in these sets the same? If not, which set contains more elemenets? Why?

This specific representation encouraged students to realize that it is possible to match each element in the first set with a corresponding element in the second set (for instance, 1 with 1^2, 2 with 2^2, etc.; in general, n is matched with n^2). They consequently correctly concluded that these two sets have the same number of elements.

Each student was then asked to examine his or her answers to the two tasks and encouraged to notice their identity. Tirosh and Tsamir (1996) reported that the use of the conflict approach in this case resulted in improvement in students' responses to the first task.

Stavy and Berkovitz (1980) used the conflict approach as a basis for teaching children in grade 4 quantitative aspects of the concept of temperature. To create the conflict, they used the two tasks related to temperature described in Chapter 1. They first presented the children with the quantitative task, namely, with three cups containing equal amounts of water with the same numerical temperature value (30°C in each cup). Then the water from two of the cups was poured into a fourth, empty cup. The children were asked to compare the temperature of the water in the fourth combined cup with that in the third cup. The majority of the participants claimed, in line with the intuitive rule "More A (amount of water)–More B (temperature)," that the temperature of the water in the combined cup was 60°C. Then the students were presented with an essentially identical qualitative task, in which the temperature of water in the three cups was not given in numbers but was verbally described as being equally warm. The researchers knew, from previous studies, that this task tends to elicit the correct response that the temperatures are equal. Then the examiner pointed out to the children that the two tasks involved the same physical situation and reminded them of the discrepancy in their answers to the quantitative and qualitative tasks. Children were asked to choose which of their answers was correct. This intervention resulted in a dramatic increase in the percentages of correct responses by the participants.

The last two cases involved situations in which students were confronted with two essentially similar tasks, one known to activate an intuitive rule, resulting in an incorrect response, and the other known to trigger a correct response. Attention was then drawn to the fact that the two tasks were essentially identical but that students' responses to them had clashed with each other. Students were then asked to reconsider their initial responses to both tasks.

Extreme Cases

In the next case, the task that triggered a correct response was designed so that it described an extreme condition for which a correct judgment was practically unavoidable. Extreme cases were used in several studies (e.g., Dembo et al., 1997; Zietsman & Clement, 1997). Dembo and colleagues (1997) called this type of conflict teaching method "the logic of limits" and used it to help the participants surmount incorrect responses in geometry, particularly those that involved conceptions of area and perimeter. They presented students aged 12 to 18 with a series of tasks, each of which involved a given geometric figure; then they transformed it, in front of the subjects, into another figure, keeping the perimeter the same. The students were then asked to compare the areas of the two figures (for instance, a square was transformed into a diamond, a circle into an ellipse). Dembo and colleagues (1997) reported that many of the students at these grade levels claimed that "same perimeter–same area." Clearly, this response is in line with the intuitive rule "Same A–Same B" (see the related description in Chapter 2).

Dembo and colleagues (1997) asked students to imagine what would happen to the respective areas of two shapes (square and circle) if the transformations were taken to their extremes. The experimenter said, "Try to imagine me continuing the actions that changed this shape into another [square into diamond and circle into ellipse]. What will happen: Will the area remain the same, will it increase or decrease?" They predicted that imagining the end state in which the area became zero would elicit the intuition that the area must be decreasing throughout the transformation, and that this conclusion would clash with the incorrect responses that the area remains equal throughout the transformation. They found that students trained in the logic of limits significantly outperformed the control group.

This same approach could be used to help students overcome incorrect responses in other domains. Let us refer, for instance, to the task related to the sweetness of two sugarwater solutions. We have shown (Chapter 2) that students tended to claim that the two sugarwater solutions containing the same amount of sugar (1 teaspoon in each cup) have the same concentration (sweetness), regardless of the amount of water in the solution (one cup of water in one solution and half a cup of water in the other). An extreme case here could consist of presenting the students with essentially the same task:

> Imagine putting a teaspoon of sugar into a aquarium and putting a teaspoon of sugar into a cup full of water. Will the sweetness of the water in the aquarium be the same/sweeter/less sweet than the sweetness of the water in the cup?

Here, students are forced to acknowledge the role of the water in this situation. Clearly, it is impossible to ignore the huge perceptual differences between the amounts of water in a cup and in an aquarium.

Both teaching by analogy and the conflict teaching approach use research-based knowledge about students' contradictory judgments about externally different but essentially similar tasks. In the cases described above, the application of these methods resulted in suppressing the effects of the intuitive rules and, consequently, in an increase in correct responses. We are not arguing that the applications of these methods always result in success. Further research is needed to determine the conditions under which each of these methods is effective.

Attention to Relevant Variables

Another teaching method that could be used to help students overcome the effects of the intuitive rules is to draw their attention to relevant variables that they tend to disregard when solving a given problem. Consider, for instance, students' tendency to claim that if Nancy saves 10% of her salary and Barry saves 5% of his salary, she saves more money. This response is in line with the intuitive rule "More A (percent)–More B (amount of saving)." In this case, the teacher could first suggest that the students use specific examples to test their predictions. Then, if the students assume that Nancy's and Barry's salaries are the same (in which case, an answer in line with the intuitive rule "More A–More B" is correct), the teacher could discuss situations in which their salaries are not the same, particularly those in which Barry's salary is larger than Nancy's. Here, the students' attention would be drawn to the fact that the salary as well as the percent determines the amount saved.

A somewhat similar method was applied by Stavy (1981). In this study, students in grades 2 to 4 were presented with the following three tasks:

1. Compare the taste of two sugarwater solutions containing the same amounts of sugar (1 teaspoon) but different amounts of water (a full cup and half a cup).
2. Compare the temperature of two different amounts of water (a full cup and half a cup) heated by the same heat sources (one candle for each cup) for the same length of time.
3. Compare the taste of equal-sized bites from two different-sized pieces of bread (one piece and half a piece) spread with the same amount of chocolate spread (1 teaspoon).

Students who gave incorrect responses of the type "Same A (amount of sugar, number of candles, amount of chocolate spread)–Same B (sweetness, temperature, taste)" disregarded the effects of the other variable (amount of water, amount of water, and size of piece of bread, respectively). They were then asked to prepare two different concentrations of saltwater: one very salty, like the water in the Dead Sea, and the other less salty, like the water in the Mediterranean. They were first presented with two cups, containing the same amount of water, and a container full of salt. All participants suggested putting a certain amount of salt in one cup and more salt in the other. This task, in line with the intuitive rule "More A (salt)–More B (salinity)," was easy for all participants.

The same participants were presented, once again, with the same task. They were asked to prepare two different concentrations of saltwater: one very salty, like the water in the Dead Sea, and the other less salty, like the water in the Mediterranean. This time, however, they were presented with two cups, each containing 1 teaspoon of salt, and a container of water. Some of the students immediately claimed that it is impossible to create different concentrations of saltwater because the amounts of salt are the same. Other participants suggested transferring some of the salt from one cup to the other. Still others suggested dissolving the salt in one cup and pouring half of it to the other cup, which already contained salt, thereby making the solution in the second cup saltier. To encourage the students to appreciate the relevance of the amount of water in this situation and to understand its role, the teacher defined the following "rules of the game":

1. Salt could not be added to any cup.
2. Salt is not to be moved from one cup to another.
3. Saltwater is not to be moved from one cup to another.

As a result, some children started to think of the role of the water in the situation; they suggested adding half a cup of water to one cup and a full cup to the other. Interestingly, this intervention resulted in a significant improvement not only in students' responses to the saltwater task, but also to the other three, previously mentioned tasks (sugarwater, temperature, bread with chocolate spread). Participants related, in these responses, to the role of the two relevant variables.

All interventions described so far resulted in suppressing the effects of an intuitive rule. Each and every such intervention should be followed by related formal explanations, proofs, definitions, and other aspects of the relevant scientific framework. Such formal knowledge may assist students in controlling the effects of the intuitive rules.

At the beginning of this chapter we raised the following questions:

> How can teachers use their knowledge about intuitive rules to improve science and mathematics education? What can they do?

We have so far suggested several teaching methods to help students overcome the effects of intuitive rules. Now we describe how some of our colleagues who were acquainted with the theory of intuitive rules used this knowledge in mathematics and science instruction.

OVERCOMING THE EFFECTS OF THE INTUITIVE RULES: USING RELATED KNOWLEDGE IN INSTRUCTION

We interviewed four colleagues, all of whom work in our department: a mathematics educator, a chemistry educator, and two physics educators. All had participated in several staff seminars in which the intuitive rules theory was presented and discussed. The mathematics educator (PT) and one of the physics educators (MM) are teacher educators. The chemistry educator (RB) and the second physics educator (SL) teach in schools and are also involved in inservice teacher education. Some days before the interviews, these four colleagues were asked to think about the following two general issues:

1. Please consider the impact of your acquaintance with the intuitive rules theory on your teaching.
2. Do you think that your knowledge about intuitive rules affects your students? If so, in what ways?

We briefly describe the interviews with each of these four colleagues.

The Mathematics Educator (PT)

PT teaches mathematics method courses to prospective middle and high school mathematics and science teachers. She has a rich experience in teaching mathematics both in high schools and in a teachers college. At the beginning of the interview, PT explained that after being exposed to the intuitive rules theory, she decided to develop a special course on the intuitive rules (12 meetings of 90 minutes each) for first-year prospective mathematics and science middle school teachers. She cooperated with the science teacher of the same prospective teachers, who was also acquainted with the intuitive rules.

> *PT*: We [the science educator of my class and I] developed an Intuitive Rules Theory Course (IRTC) for prospective teachers of mathematics and science in middle school. The main aims of this course were (1) to introduce the intuitive rules theory by demonstrating the strong effect of the rules on participants' *own responses* to mathematics and science tasks, (2) to raise prospective teachers' awareness of possible effects of the intuitive rules on their future students' responses to mathematics and science tasks, and (3) to train teachers to plan instruction taking account of the intuitive rules.
>
> *Question*: Can you please describe the Intuitive Rules Theory Course?
>
> *PT*: In the first two meetings of the course, the participants responded to two questionnaires: The Prospective Teachers Questionnaire (PTQ) and the Student Thinking Questionnaire (STQ).
>
> The PTQ included 40 comparison tasks in mathematics and science known to elicit responses of the type "More A–More B" and "Same A–Same B." All tasks related to topics included in the middle school mathematics and science curricula. The applications of the intuitive rules yielded correct responses to some of these tasks and incorrect responses to others.
>
> My prediction was that my students would use the intuitive rules to respond to at least some of the tasks and would come up with incorrect responses.
>
> The STQ included three parts, all related to didactic implications of the intuitive rules. Part 1 of the STQ presented respondents with 10 comparison tasks, with several common students responses to each task. The correct response was marked as such.

Participants were asked to suggest possible reasons for each response (including the correct one). In part 2, comparison tasks were given and the assignment was to predict common student responses to these tasks and to list possible sources for each of these responses. Part 3 presented comparison tasks, and respondents were asked to provide reasons for presenting/not presenting each task in their future classes. I designed this questionnaire to include some "easy" and some "difficult" tasks (i.e., tasks whose correct answer was in line with an intuitive rule was deemed "easy," while a task whose correct answer contradicted an intuitive rule was likely to be "difficult"). Information about the level of difficulty of the tasks was not disclosed to my students.

Question: So far you have described the two questionnaires. How did you use them in the course?

PT: The prospective teachers' responses to the PTQ and to the STQ were used both for the definition of the intuitive rules and for a discussion of their possible impact on their own as well as their future students' responses to comparison tasks.

With respect to the PTQ, my analyses of students' responses confirm my prediction that many of their responses would be in line with the intuitive rules. I then divided the class into small groups. Each group received six to seven comparison tasks from the questionnaire. Their assignment was to discuss their responses and to agree on a generally accepted solution to each of these tasks. A representative of each group reported to the entire class on the work of his or her group, including the initial responses of each member, the discussions that took place in the group, and the final conclusions. Many groups reported that they could not reach an agreement. Among those that reached agreement, some groups agreed on an incorrect solution, in line with an intuitive rule.

The entire class was then asked to look at various textbooks and other resources to find out the correct solutions (as any teacher should do when unsure of a certain solution). In the next lessons, I discussed the formal answers to the mathematics tasks with my students, and the science teacher did the same for the science tasks.

PT explained that this part served as a way to discuss many middle school science and mathematics concepts and to strengthen the prospective teachers' formal knowledge. No less important, from her perspective, was the fact that the prospective teachers themselves experienced the effect of the intuitive rules on their own responses. She then explained how she used prospective teachers' responses to these questionnaires to promote the discussion on the intuitive rules.

> In the following lesson I posed the following question: *What could be the causes of your incorrect responses?*
> The prospective teachers noticed that responses of the types "More A–More B" and "Same A–Same B" often occurred both in their own work (in their responses to the PTQ) and in that of their future students (in the STQ). We then related each type of response to a specific task structure, introducing the intuitive rules "More A–More B" and "Same A–Same B." My students also noticed that sometimes the application of these rules yielded correct responses but that often they yielded incorrect ones. They were then asked to read several related articles [Stavy & Tirosh, 1996; Tirosh & Stavy, 1996, 1999], to prepare brief reports on the main issues, and to present them in class.

PT explained that the prospective teachers were impressed by the idea that many of their own and their future students' common responses were determined by the structure of the tasks, not by their content. She mentioned that it was quite difficult for them to accept this idea. PT then discussed possible implications of the theory of intuitive rules for instruction:

> I found that prospective teachers tended to argue that correct responses result from formal knowledge only (such responses were typical even in tasks when an answer in line with the intuitive rule was consistent with the formal answer). We discussed this issue in class, showing that correct answers might evolve from the application of intuitive rules and are not necessarily based on formal knowledge. In their responses to part 3 of the STQ, many participants expressed their belief that "difficult" tasks, which are expected to trigger incorrect intuitive responses, should not be presented in class. The ideas that it is not fair to present students with "difficult," counterintuitive problems and that teachers should choose problems that trigger success and avoid failure were repeatedly expressed both in writing and in the discussions. To show that "difficult" tasks could be used in teaching a given topic, we discussed various teaching methods that make use of our knowledge about "easy" and "difficult" tasks (e.g., conflict teaching, teaching by analogy).
> Prospective teachers were then asked to work in pairs to

search the curriculum for problems that were likely to trigger the application of the intuitive rules. They were asked to classify each of these tasks as either "easy" or "difficult" and to justify their choice. They then tried these problems with a group of middle school students. They analyzed students' responses in terms of their correctness, students' dependence on intuitive rules, and the predicted degree of difficulty of each task. Finally, each pair presented its findings in class.

PT noted that searching the curriculum for problems likely to trigger the application of the intuitive rules was an extremely difficult task for the participants, even for those who showed a satisfactory understanding of the intuitive rules. She also commented that the sessions with middle school students contributed a great deal to participants' attitudes toward the intuitive rules: They were impressed by their explanatory and predictive powers.

At the end of the interview, PT expressed her strong belief that awareness of the intuitive rules is very important for teachers. She thought they should use this theory to analyze their students' responses to various tasks in different contexts (e.g., mathematics, science, everyday life), to assess the difficulty of given tasks, and to aid in designing instruction. She noted that this course also gave her, as a prospective teacher educator, an opportunity to reconsider various content domains in the middle school curriculum from a fresh, unusual angle.

PT was the only educator we interviewed who developed a special course on the intuitive rules. MM, the prospective physics teacher educator, used his knowledge about the theory of intuitive rules in a different manner.

The Physics Educator (MM)

For more than 20 years, MM has been teaching a physics methods course to students majoring in physics (toward a B.Sc. degree) who are also earning a teacher certificate in high school physics.

At the beginning of the interview, MM described three stages in his professional development: the subject-matter stage, the alternative-conception stage, and the intuitive-rules stage.

> *MM*: At the beginning of my career as a physics educator, I was convinced that my job was to teach the usual high school subject matter from a didactic viewpoint. This was the first stage of my career, during which I *emphasized only the subject matter*.
>
> Later on, I was surprised to realize that even my students, who all had a B.Sc. in physics, still had difficulties in understand-

ing some topics. Consequently, I became interested in research related to prospective teachers and high school students' alternative conceptions. I understood that, as a teacher educator, I should "know the enemy" and that my students, who will be teachers, should also be acquainted with their enemies. As a result, I moved to the second stage in my professional development: *emphasizing students' alternative conceptions.*

My problem at this stage was that I had to relate to many independent, unrelated alternative conceptions. I had no means to predict these alternative conceptions. The fact that I, my friends (some of whom are distinguished physics professors), my students, and their future students all fall into similar traps led me to suspect that there must be a reason behind this.

The intuitive rules theory led me to a third stage in my professional development: *emphasizing the role of the intuitive rules.*

Question: How does your knowledge of the intuitive rules affect your teaching?

MM: Instead of presenting the materials as such, I tend to begin the instruction related to a specific topic with problems that have the potential to activate a certain incorrect response, in line with an intuitive rule. Then I ask the students to predict the answer, and, as expected, at least some of them will answer incorrectly (e.g., "More A–More B"). Then we do an experiment that demonstrates the correct answer. My students (the future teachers) are then faced with the fact that their initial answers were incorrect. We then discuss the formal physics explanation. Next, I ask them to explain what caused their incorrect responses. They tend to give explanations such as "I was mistakenly thinking that the distance is relevant here, and that led me to argue that the larger distance would take more time."

We then asked MM if he explicitly discusses the intuitive rules theory with his students.

For several lessons, I usually do not talk explicitly about the intuitive rules, but I do show them, in each lesson, specific instances of an intuitive rule, and gradually they see the similarities in their responses. Then we talk about the intuitive rules.

My feeling is that after seeing some cases, they themselves will be more cautious in the next case. They will be more suspicious toward responses of the type "More A–More B," "Same A–Same B," and will critically examine them.

One of my goals, as a teacher of future teachers, is to raise their awareness of the regularities in common mistakes. I hope that with their future students they will do what I have been doing with them. The whole project of the intuitive rules really interested and motivated my students. They look for instances. And as a matter of fact, it motivates me as well. I also look for instances of these rules.

The Chemistry Educator (RB)

RB uses her knowledge about the intuitive rules both in her role as a high school chemistry teacher and as an inservice high school teacher trainer in chemistry. At the beginning of the interview, RB explained that her awareness of the intuitive rules has substantially affected her instruction in both her functions. She first discussed high school teaching, clarifying how she uses this knowledge to react to students' responses:

RB: I clearly see the effect of the intuitive rule "More A–More B" in topics involving intensive quantities (e.g., temperature, concentration, pH) or inverse ratios. When teaching these topics, if one of my students gives an incorrect answer in line with this rule, I explain to the entire class that this response is an intuitive, natural one without mentioning the correctness/incorrectness of the response. I emphasize that although it intuitively seems correct, we still have to test it. We then search for a way (e.g., an experiment) to test the validity of the student's response. Sometimes I draw an analogy to daily life to convince my students that their responses are correct (or incorrect). I'll provide a specific example.

In one of my classes I asked the following question: Consider 1 gram of each of the following substances—Na_2O, Li_2O, and K_2O. Which of these samples of substances contains more ions? Many students incorrectly answered that "the sample of the substance with the higher molecular mass contains the larger number of ions." Then I used an elevator by analogy. I clarified that the maximum allowed weight in this elevator is 1,000 kg (resembling the amount of substance—1 gram) and that this elevator could contain a larger number of people (number of ions) of lower weight (lower molecular mass) than of higher weight (higher molecular mass).

Question: Do you use your knowledge about other intuitive rules as well?

RB: Certainly. For example, the intuitive rule "Everything can be divided" makes it difficult for students to use the particulate theory of matter. Even students who know that matter is composed of particles sometimes do not use this knowledge and give incorrect responses in line with this intuitive rule.

When dealing with several topics—such as radioactive decomposition, serial dilution of solutions, the relationship between micro and macro properties of substances—I raise a question related to this rule, such as: Will the process of radioactive decomposition come to a halt? We then discuss incorrect responses (the process will go on forever) in light of the particulate theory of matter, again stressing the impact of the intuitive tendency to answer in an incorrect way.

In this case, RB was the initiator of a discussion on the intuitive tendency to assume that a given chemical process is infinite. She intentionally asked a question that triggered the use of the intuitive rule and, then, discussed the intuitive responses in light of the particulate theory of matter. RB explained that she also uses her knowledge of the intuitive rules to plan sequences of instruction:

RB: I try to start teaching a given topic with examples for which an intuitive rule leads to a correct response, that is, supports the related scientific knowledge. For instance: The stronger the attraction forces between the particles, the higher the boiling point of this substance. Later, I present examples for which the use of this rule leads to incorrect responses, thereby showing the boundaries of the application of this rule. For instance, in respect to attraction forces between particles, as stated above, the rule "More A–More B" holds for the boiling point but not for the freezing point.

Question: How does your knowledge of the intuitive rules affect your instruction in teacher education?

RB: Teachers should be aware of the intuitive rules and their possible impact on students responses. They should understand that the intuitive rules are the sources of many of the difficulties students have in understanding certain topics. They should know how to design instruction that considers the role of the intuitive rules and how to react to incorrect responses.

RB made it clear that she does not explicitly talk about the intuitive rules with high school students. However, she emphasized that, in her opinion, introducing the intuitive rules to teachers is a must.

The Physics Teacher (SL)

SL is a research assistant in our department and also teaches physics in high school. At the beginning of the interview, she discussed her own concerns about the intuitive rules.

> *SL*: I heard from you about the intuitive rules and was not sure that these rules affected my own or my students' responses to physics tasks. However, after hearing from you, I became more sensitive to such responses and I was surprised to find that in every single topic and almost in each lesson, many of my students' responses were of the type "Same A–Same B" and "More A–More B" (e.g., same force–same acceleration, same electrical charge–same electrical field, the heavier–the faster). So, I realized that the intuitive rules were indeed there.
>
> *Question*: Can you please describe whether and how this realization affected your instruction?
>
> *SL*: I can describe two steps in this process. At the beginning, I used this knowledge to identify and analyze students' responses and to plan my instruction. For instance, when teaching projectile motion, I started with a demonstration: I used two identical balls that were simultaneously released from the same apparatus—V_0 of one of these balls was zero, and the second was horizontally projected with $V_0 > 0$. I asked the class to predict, before the demonstration, whether the two balls would reach the ground at the same time or not and, if not, which ball would reach the ground first. About 50% of the class predicted that the first ball would be the first one to hit the ground, because "the longer the distance–the longer the time." Then the demonstration was carried out, and my students were surprised to see the results. This enabled me to show that the first and second balls indeed hit the ground together and that falling time is determined only by the height.
>
> This was the first step. At this stage I did not discuss these rules with my students.
>
> *Question*: Can you describe the second step?
>
> *SL*: That's when I decided to raise my students' awareness of the role of the intuitive rules in their thinking. I believe that such awareness could serve as a "red light," namely, as a tool for them to identify responses of the type "More A–More B" or "Same A–Same B" and to start questioning their validity. My goal, as a teacher, is to encourage my students to critically examine their re-

sponses and to test whether these responses are in line with the
situation and with the rules of physics. Awareness of the role of
the intuitive rules in their thinking could be used as a tool to promote such behavior.

Question: Can you share with us what you did with your students to
achieve this aim?

In her response to this question, SL told us that she explicitly presented
the intuitive rules theory in her class. In her presentation, she used many
examples from physics and some examples from mathematics. She related
to each of these examples from two viewpoints: that of the subject matter
and that of the intuitive rules theory. Later, she asked her students to respond
in writing to the following question: Do you think your knowledge about
the intuitive rules can assist you? If yes, explain how. If not, explain why
not.

SL reported that her students showed great interest in the intuitive rules.
All of them were convinced that the intuitive rules affect their responses to
tasks, and they provided examples of use of the rules. They explained that
knowledge about the intuitive rules is very important to them and to their
teachers. A typical response was: "Now I know about the intuitive rules,
and I know that I should beware of the impact of them on my responses. I
now know that I should test my responses via calculation or in other ways
before giving the answer."

SL commented that, at this point, she did not have information about
the extent to which knowledge about the intuitive rules indeed served as a
"red light" for her students. She believed it did.

In all four interviews, our colleagues stated that acquaintance with the
intuitive rules theory affected their instruction. They reported that knowledge of this theory encouraged them to reflect on and reconsider their instruction and their responses to students' correct and incorrect answers. The
issue of exposing their own students to the intuitive rules theory was also
addressed. All four clearly stated that intuitive rules theory is "a must" for
teachers.

At the beginning of this chapter, we suggested that teachers should be
aware of the role of the intuitive rules in students' thinking. We described
several ways to implement knowledge about the intuitive rules theory in
teaching science and mathematics. The interviews with our four colleagues
showed how their knowledge about the intuitive rules was actually applied
in instruction.

References

Index

About the Author

of mathematics. New York: Cambridge University Press. (Original work published 1925)

Hirstein, J. (1981). The second area assessment in mathematics: Area and volume. *Mathematics Teacher, 74,* 704–708.

Hoffer, A. R., & Hoffer, S. A. K. (1992). Geometry and visual thinking. In T. R. Post (Ed.), *Teaching mathematics in grades K–8: Research-based methods* (2nd ed.). Boston: Allyn & Bacon.

Inhelder, B., & Piaget, J. (1958). *The growth of logical thinking: From childhood to adolescence.* New York: Basic Books.

Jackendoff, R. (1989). What is a concept, that a person may grasp it? *Mind and Language, 4,* 68–102.

Karplus, R., Karplus, E., Formisano, M., & Paulsen, A. C. (1977). A survey of proportional reasoning and control of variables in seven countries. *Journal of Research in Science Teaching, 14,* 411–417.

Kopelevich, S. (1997). *Wrong use of the intuitive rule: "More of A–more of B" in power.* Unpublished master's thesis, Tel-Aviv University, Tel Aviv, Israel. (in Hebrew)

Langer, J. (1969). Disequilibrium as a source of development. In P. H. Mussen, J. Langer, & M. Lovington (Eds.), *Trends and issues in developmental psychology* (pp. 22–37). New York: Holt, Rinehart & Winston.

Larkin, J., & Rainhard, B. (1984). Research methodology for studying how people think. *Journal of Research in Science Teaching, 21,* 235–254.

Lawson, A. E. (1995). *Science teaching and the development of thinking.* Belmont, CA: Wadsworth.

Levin, I. (1977). The development of time concepts in young children. Reasoning about duration. *Child Development, 48,* 435–444.

Levin, I. (1979). Interference of time-related and unrelated cues with duration comparisons of young children: Analysis of Piaget's formulation of the relation of time and speed. *Child Development, 50,* 469–477.

Levin, I. (1982). The nature and development of time concepts in children: The effects of interfering cues. In W. J. Friedman (Ed.), *The developmental psychology of time* (pp. 47–85). New York: Academic Press.

Linchevsky, L. (1985). *The meaning attributed by elementary school teachers to terms they use in teaching mathematics and geometry.* Unpublished doctoral dissertation, Hebrew University, Jerusalem, Israel. (in Hebrew)

Lindsay, P., & Norman, D. (1972). *Human information processing: An introduction to psychology.* New York: Academic Press.

Linn, M. C., Layman, J., & Nachmias, R. (1987). Cognitive consequences of microcomputer-based learning: Graphing skills development. *Journal of Contemporary Psychology, 12,* 244–253.

Livne, T. (1996). *Examination of high school students' difficulties in understanding the change in surface area, volume and surface area/volume ratio with the change in size and/or shape of a body.* Unpublished master's thesis, Tel-Aviv University, Tel Aviv, Israel. (in Hebrew)

McClosky, M. (1983a). Naive theories of motion. In D. Gentner & A. L. Stevens (Eds.), *Mental models* (pp. 299–324). Hillsdale, NJ: Erlbaum.

McClosky, M. (1983b, April). Intuitive physics. *Scientific American,* p. 114.

McMahon, T. A., & Bonner, J. T. (1983). *On size and life.* New York: Scientific American Library, Scientific American Books.

Megged, H. (1978). *The development of the concept of density among children ages 6–16.* Unpublished master's thesis, Tel Aviv University, Tel Aviv, Israel. (in Hebrew)

Mehler, J., & Bever, T. G. (1967). Cognitive capacity of very young children. *Science, 158,* 141–142.

Mendel, N. (1998). *The intuitive rule "Same of A, same of B": The case of comparison of rectangles.* Unpublished manuscript. Tel Aviv University, Tel Aviv, Israel. (in Hebrew)

Morabia, D. (1990). *Difficulties in applying the principle of the "independence of motions" among high school students.* Unpublished master's thesis, Tel Aviv University, Tel Aviv, Israel. (in Hebrew)

Mueller, I. (1981). *Philosophy of mathematics and deductive structure in Euclid's elements.* Cambridge, MA: MIT Press.

Myers, S. (1998). *Effects of conceptual conflicts on using the intuitive rule "More of A–more of B" in 8th grade students.* Unpublished master's thesis, Tel Aviv University, Tel Aviv, Israel. (in Hebrew)

National Council of Teachers of Mathematics. (1989). *Curriculum and evaluation standard for school mathematics.* Reston, VA: Author.

Nesher, P. (1986). Are mathematical understanding and algorithmic performance related? *For the Learning of Mathematics, 6,* 2–9.

Noelting, G. (1980a). The development of proportional reasoning and the ratio concept: Part I—Differentiation of stages. *Educational Studies in Mathematics, 11,* 217–253.

Noelting, G. (1980b). The development of proportional reasoning and the ratio concept: Part II—Problem structure at successive stages: Problem solving strategies and the mechanism of adaptive restructuring. *Educational Studies in Mathematics, 11,* 331–363.

Noss, R., & Hoyles, C. (1996). *Windows on mathematical meanings: Learning cultures and computers.* Dordrecht, The Netherlands: Kluwer.

Novak, J. D. (Ed.). (1983). *Proceedings of the International Seminar: Misconceptions in Science and Mathematics.* Ithaca, NY: Cornell University Press.

Novak, J. D. (Ed.). (1987). *Proceedings of the Second International Seminar: Misconceptions and Educational Strategies in Science and Mathematics.* Ithaca, NY; Cornell University Press.

Novak, J. D., & Gowin, D. B. (Eds.). (1984). *Learning how to learn.* Cambridge, England: Cambridge University Press.

Nunes, T., Schliemann, A. D., & Carraher, D. W. (1993). *Street mathematics and school mathematics.* Cambridge, England: Cambridge University Press.

Nunez, R. (1991). A 3-dimension conceptual space of transformations for the study of the intuition of infinity in plane geometry. In F. Furinghetti (Ed.), *Proceed-*

ings of the Fifteenth Conference for the Psychology of Mathematics Education (Vol. 3; pp. 362–368). Assisi, Italy: Program Committee of the 15th PME Conference.

Osborne, R., & Freyberg, P. (1985). *Learning in science: The implications of children's science.* Auckland, New Zealand: Heinemann.

Perkins, D. N., & Simmons, R. (1988). Patterns of misunderstanding: An integrative model for science, math, and programming. *Review of Education Research, 58,* 303–326.

Pfundt, H. (1981). Pre-instructional conception about substances and transformation of substances. In W. Jung, H. Pfundt, & C. V. Rhonock (Eds.), *Problems concerning students' representation of physics and chemistry knowledge* (pp. 320–341). Ludwigsburg, Germany: Frankfurt University.

Pfundt, H., & Duit, R. (1994). *Bibliography: Students' alternative frameworks and science education* (IPN Reports in brief). Germany: University of Kiel.

Piaget, J. (1965). *The child's conception of number.* New York: Norton. (Original work published 1952)

Piaget, J. (1968). *On the development of memory and identity.* Barre, MA: Clark University Press.

Piaget, J. (1969). *The child's conception of time.* New York: Basic Books.

Piaget, J. (1980). *Experiments in contradiction.* Chicago: University of Chicago Press.

Piaget, J., Grize, J. B., Szeminska, A., & Bang, B. (1968). *Epistemologie et psychologie de la fonction* [Epistemology and psychology of the function]. Paris: Presses Universitaires de France.

Piaget, J., & Inhelder, B. (1963). *The child's conception of space.* London: Routledge & Kegan Paul.

Piaget, J., & Inhelder, B. (1974). *The child's construction of quantity.* London: Routledge & Kegan Paul.

Piaget, J., Inhelder, B., & Szeminska, A. (1960). *The child's conception of geometry.* London: Routledge & Kegan Paul.

Pitkethly, A., & Hunting, R. (1996). A review of recent research in the area of initial fraction concepts. *Educational Studies in Mathematics, 30,* 5–38.

Poincaré, H. (1906). *La Science et l'hypothese* [Science and the assumption]. Paris: Flammarion.

Rapaport, A. (1998). *Use of the intuitive rule: "More of A–more of B" in comparing algebraic expressions.* Unpublished master's thesis, Tel Aviv University, Tel Aviv, Israel. (in Hebrew)

Ravia, N. (1992). *Inconsistencies in the perception of the concepts heat and temperature (9th grade).* Unpublished master's thesis, Tel Aviv University, Tel Aviv, Israel. (in Hebrew)

Rojhany, L. (1997). *The use of the intuitive rule "The more of A, the more of B": The case of comparison of angles.* Unpublished master's thesis, Tel Aviv University, Tel Aviv, Israel. (in Hebrew)

Ronen, E. (in press). *The intuitive rule "same A–same B": The case of overgeneral-*

ization of the conservation schema. Unpublished doctoral dissertation, Tel Aviv University, Tel Aviv, Israel. (in Hebrew)

Schrage, G. L. (1983). (Mis-)interpretation of stochastic models. In R. Scholz (Ed.), *Decision making under uncertainty* (pp. 351–361). Amsterdam: North-Holland.

Segal, N. (in press). *Exploring the role of cognitive conflict in conservation tasks: The case of "same A–same B."* Unpublished master's thesis, Tel Aviv University, Tel Aviv, Israel. (in Hebrew)

Sere, M. G. (1982). A study of some frameworks used by pupils aged 11–13 years in the interpretation of air pressure. *European Journal of Science Education, 4,* 299–309.

Shayer, M., & Adey, P. (1981). *Towards a science of science teaching: Cognitive development and curriculum demand.* London: Heinemann.

Shohet, N. (1994). *The dominance of the natural numbers in high school students reference to algebra.* Unpublished master's thesis, Tel Aviv University, Tel Aviv, Israel. (in Hebrew)

Shultz, T., Dover, A., & Amsel, E. (1979). The logical and empirical bases of conservation judgments. *Cognition, 7,* 99–123.

Smith, J., diSessa, A., & Roschelle, J. (1993). Misconceptions reconceived: A constructivist analysis of knowledge in transition. *The Journal of the Learning Science, 3*(2), 115–163.

Spelke, E. S. (1991). Physical knowledge in infancy: Reflections on Piaget's theory. In S. Carey & R. Gelman (Eds.), *The epigenesis of mind: Essays in biology and cognition* (pp. 133–169). Hillsdale, NJ: Erlbaum.

Stavy, R. (1981). Teaching inverse function via the concentration of salt water solution. *Archives de Psychologie, 49,* 267–287.

Stavy, R., & Berkovitz, B. (1980). Cognitive conflict as a basis for teaching quantitative aspects of the concept of temperature. *Science Education, 64,* 679–692.

Stavy, R., & Stachel, D. (1985). Children's conception of changes in the state of matter: From solid to liquid. *Archives de Psychologie, 3,* 331–344.

Stavy, R., Strauss, S., Orpaz, N., & Carmi, G. (1982). U-shaped behavioral growth in ratio comparisons, or that's funny I would not have thought you were U-ish. In S. Strauss & R. Stavy (Eds.), *U-shaped behavioral growth* (pp. 11–36). New York: Academic Press.

Stavy, R., & Tirosh, D. (1992). Overgeneralization in mathematics and science: The effect of external similarity. *International Journal of Mathematical Education in Science and Technology, 32,* 229–248.

Stavy, R., & Tirosh, D. (1993a). Subdivision processes in mathematics and science. *Journal of Research in Science Teaching, 30,* 579–586.

Stavy, R., & Tirosh, D. (1993b). When analogy is perceived as such. *Journal of Research in Science Teaching, 30,* 1229–1239.

Stavy, R., & Tirosh, D. (1996). Intuitive rules in mathematics and science: The case of "the more of A the more of B." *International Journal of Science Education, 18,* 653–667.

Stern, E., & Mevarech, Z. R. (1991). *When familiar context does not facilitate math-*

ematical understanding. Unpublished manuscript, Max Planck Institute, Berlin, Germany.

Strauss, S. (1972). Inducing cognitive development and learning: A review of short-term training studies: The organisimic-developmental approach. *Cognition, 1,* 105.

Strauss, S. (1982). (Ed.). *U-shaped behavioral growth.* New York: Academic Press.

Strauss, S., & Stavy, R. (1982). U-shaped behavioral growth: Implications for theories of development. In W. W. Hartup (Ed.), *Review of child development research* (pp. 547–599). Chicago: University of Chicago Press.

Strauss, S., Stavy, R., & Orpaz, N. (1977). *The development of the concept of temperature.* Unpublished manuscript, Tel Aviv University, Tel Aviv, Israel.

Svensson, L. (1989). The conceptualisation of cases of physical motion. *European Journal of Psychology of Education, 4,* 529–545.

Tall, D. O. (1981). Intuition of infinity. *Mathematics in School, 10*(3), 30–33.

Tall, D. O., & Vinner, S. (1981). Concept image and concept definition with particular reference to limits and continuity. *Educational Studies in Mathematics, 12,* 151–169.

Thijs, G. D., & van den Berg, E. (1995). Cultural factors in the origin and remediation of alternative conceptions in physics. *Science and Education, 4,* 317–347.

Tinbergen, N. (1955). *The study of instinct.* Oxford: Clarendon Press.

Tirosh, D. (1985). *The intuition of infinity and its relevance for mathematical education.* Unpublished doctoral thesis, Tel Aviv University, Tel Aviv, Israel. (in Hebrew)

Tirosh, D. (1990). Inconsistencies in students' mathematical constructs. *Focus on Learning Problems in Mathematics, 12,* 111–129.

Tirosh, D., & Stavy, R. (1992). Students' ability to confine their application of knowledge: The case of mathematics and science. *School Science and Mathematics, 92,* 353–358.

Tirosh, D., & Stavy, R. (1996). Intuitive rules in science and mathematics: The case of "everything can be divided by two." *International Journal of Science Education, 18,* 669–683.

Tirosh, D., & Stavy, R. (1999). Intuitive rules: A way to explain and predict students' reasoning. *Educational Studies in Mathematics, 38,* 51–66.

Tirosh, D., Stavy, R., & Cohen, S. (1998). Cognitive conflict and intuitive rules. *International Journal of Science Education, 20,* 1257–1269.

Tirosh, D., & Tsamir, P. (1996). The role of representations in students' intuitive thinking about infinity. *International Journal of Mathematics Education in Science and Technology, 27,* 33–40.

Tsamir, P. (1997). *Predicting students' responses when comparing vertical angles.* Unpublished manuscript, Tel Aviv University, Tel Aviv, Israel.

Tsamir, P., Tirosh, D., & Stavy, R. (1997). Intuitive rules and comparison tasks: The grasp of vertical angles. In G. A. Makrides (Ed.), *Proceedings of the First Mediterranean Conference: Mathematics Education and Applications.* Nicosia, Cyprus: Cyprus Redagogical Institute and Cyprus Mathematical Society.

Tversky, A., & Kahneman, D. (1972). Subjective probability: A judgment of representativeness. *Cognitive Psychology, 3,* 430–454.

Tytler, R. (1998a). The nature of students' informal science conceptions. *International Journal of Science Education, 20,* 901–927.

Tytler, R. (1998b). Children's conceptions of air pressure: Exploring the nature of conceptual change. *International Journal of Science Education, 20,* 929–958.

van den Heuvel-Panhuizen, M. (1994). Improvement of (didactic) assessment by improvements of problems: An attempt with respect to percentages. *Educational Studies in Mathematics, 27,* 341–372.

Viennot, L. (1985). Analysing student's reasoning in science: A pragmatic view of theoretical problems. *European Journal of Science Education, 7,* 151–162.

Vosniadou, S., & Brewer, W. F. (1987). Theories of knowledge restructuring in development. *Review of Educational Research, 57,* 51–67.

Vygotsky, L. S. (1962). *Thought and language.* Cambridge, MA: MIT Press.

Walter, N. (1970). A common misconception about area. *Arithmetic Teacher, 17,* 286–289.

Weirzbicka, A. (1980). *Lingua mentalis.* New York: Academic Press.

Wiser, M., & Carey, S. (1983). When heat and temperature were one. In D. Gentner & A. L. Stevens (Eds.), *Mental models* (pp. 267–296). Hillsdale, NJ: Erlbaum.

Woodward, E., & Byrd, F. (1983). Area: Included topic, neglected concept. *School Science and Mathematics, 83,* 343–347.

Zagury, S. (1997). *Use of the intuitive rule "more of A–more of B": In ordering negative numbers.* Unpublished master's thesis, Tel Aviv University, Tel Aviv, Israel. (in Hebrew)

Zahir, A. (1997). *The use of intuitive rules in the calculation of circumference, perimeter and volume.* Unpublished master's thesis, Tel Aviv University, Tel Aviv, Israel. (in Hebrew)

Zietsman, A., & Clement, J. (1997). The role of extreme case reasoning in instruction for conceptual change. *Journal of Learning Sciences, 6,* 61–89.

Zohar, A. (1995). Reasoning about interactions between variables. *Journal of Research in Science Teaching, 32,* 1039–1063.

Index

About the Authors

Ruth Stavy is a full professor of science education in the Department of Science Education at Tel Aviv University, Israel. Before joining Tel Aviv University in 1974, she did research as a biochemist at the Weizmann Institute of Science, Rehovoth, Israel.

From 1974 through 1985 she was engaged in elementary school science curriculum development at the Israel Science Teaching Center at Tel Aviv University. She has been a member of the academic staff of Tel Aviv University since 1985. From 1993 to 1995 she served as head of the Department of Teacher Education and from 1995 through 1999 as head of the Department of Science Education. Her main interests are in students' scientific concepts, the history of science, and the role of intuitive rules in science and mathematics.

Dina Tirosh is a full professor of mathematics education in the Department of Science Education at Tel Aviv University, Israel, where she has been on the faculty since 1986. She was previously a mathematics teacher in high schools and in teachers colleges. Her main interests are in students' mathematical concepts (e.g., the development of students' understanding of the concept of infinity), teacher education and the professional development of mathematics teachers, and the role of intuitive rules in science and mathematics. She is currently the head of the Department of Science Education at Tel Aviv University.